ROBERT BURNS

Pride and Passion

Rob.t Burns was born at Alloway in the Parish of Ayr — Jan.y 25th 1759 —

Jean Armour his wife was born at Mauchline Feb.ry 27th 1767 —

Sept.r 3: 1786 were born to them twins, Robert, their eldest Son, at a quarter past Noon. & Jean, since dead at fourteen months old. — March 3. 1788 were born to them twins again, two daughters, who died within a few days after their birth. — August 18th 1789 was born to them Francis, Wallace; so named after M.rs Dunlop of Dunlop: he was born a quarter before seven, forenoon. — April 9th 1791, between three & four in the morning, was born to them William, Nicol; so named after Will.m Nicol of the High School, Edin.r —— November. 21.st 1792, at a quarter past Noon, was born to them Elizabeth, Riddel, so named after Mrs Rob.t Riddel of Glenriddel. — James Glencairn born 12th Aug.t 1794 named after the late Earl of Glencairn

Maxwell Born 26th July 1796 the day of his Fathers Funeral. so named after Dr Maxwell the Physician who attended the Poet in his last illness Inserted by W. N. Burns 9th April 1867

Family register by Robert Burns in the household Bible preserved at Burns Cottage, Alloway. This facsimile first appeared in the *Life and Works of Robert Burns* by P. Hately Waddell (Glasgow, 1867)

ROBERT BURNS
Pride and Passion
THE LIFE, TIMES AND LEGACY

Gavin Sprott

General Accident

THE NATIONAL LIBRARY OF SCOTLAND

THE NATIONAL MUSEUMS OF SCOTLAND

EDINBURGH: HMSO

The publisher has taken all reasonable steps to obtain from their copyright
holders permission to reproduce the images which appear in this volume.
Excerpts from the writings of Burns used in this book are taken from *The
Complete Works of Robert Burns* (Ayr, 1986) and *The Complete Letters of Robert
Burns* (Ayr, 1987), both edited and introduced by James A. Mackay.

British Library Cataloguing in Publication Data
A catalogue record for this book is available from the British Library.

This book is based on the exhibition 'Pride and Passion', jointly created by
the National Library of Scotland and the National Museums of Scotland, in
association with the National Galleries of Scotland, and first shown in the
Royal Museum of Scotland, Edinburgh, from 8 June to 15 September 1996.
Both exhibition and book are generously supported by

General Accident

THE AUTHOR
Gavin Sprott is currently
Curator of the Scottish Agricultural Museum, Edinburgh.
He is the author of several books, including *Robert Burns, Farmer.*

Design by James Hutcheson
Set in Adobe Garamond
The device which appears under each chapter heading was used in the first
edition of Burns's poems, published in Kilmarnock in 1786.
Cover and title page illustration: Burns by John Buego,
after Alexander Nasmyth

ISBN 0 11 495744 4

CONTENTS

ACKNOWLEDGEMENTS

IT IS A GENUINE PLEASURE to thank people for their help in the writing and production of this book.

The book reflects the pattern of 'Pride and Passion', the major Burns bicentenary exhibition mounted jointly in 1996 by the National Library of Scotland and the National Museums of Scotland, in association with the National Galleries of Scotland. I thus owe much to the stimulus and originality of thought of my fellow workers on the Curatorial Committee for the exhibition: Kenneth Dunn, Dr Kenneth Gibson and Dr William Kelly of the National Library of Scotland, and Mungo Campbell and Dr Duncan Thomson of the National Galleries of Scotland.

Representing the publishers, Alastair Fyfe Holmes and Liz Fergusson have been sure-footed and, indeed, most considerate. As the book hinges on interpretation, I value highly Jim Hutcheson's thoughtful design and Walter Ross's ingenious picture research, so ably supported by the efforts of Carol Forbes and Barbara Hegarty of the National Library of Scotland.

I am indebted to my scholarly neighbour Bob Walker for opening my eyes to the importance of the theological background (including the works of my learned kinsman George Washington Sprott of Anwoth) and likewise to Robert Cooper of the Grand Lodge of Scotland for his enlightening perspectives on Freemasonry. Hugh Cheape of the National Museums of Scotland has made valuable suggestions from his copious knowledge of, and insight into, Celtic matters.

Ann Vinnicombe's copy-editing has kept me in order and clarified the text. Dr James Mackay has been generous not only in time but in the spirit in which he has made valuable suggestions and spotted errors. Needless to say, the errors that remain are mine.

Gavin Sprott
NATIONAL MUSEUMS OF SCOTLAND

INTRODUCTION

THE STARTING POINT FOR THIS BOOK is the interpretation of a different age. Burns is deceptive. Such is the freshness of his poetry that much of it could have been written today. Yet the world is two hundred years older, and, in L. P. Hartley's now famous words from *The Go-Between*, 'the past is a foreign country: they do things differently there' – getting under the skin of it is all intelligent guesswork. But we can have a crack at it, and, for all their limitations, the insights can give a genuine sense of freshness to our understanding of Robert Burns.

The earlier biographies of Burns were united in one assertion – that the main obstacle with which Burns had to contend was himself. The image persists: Rhymer Rab the drouth, womaniser and getter of bastard weans. Another tradition, far from quarrying for the feet of clay, has Burns the unspotted hero who can do no wrong, and rears Highland Mary into Our Lady of the Tartan Sighs.

It is not the concern of this book to hold the ring in a battle over Burns's reputation. It is not a biography of Burns in a conventional sense, nor is it an expert literary assessment of his poetry. These things have been done by many and able scholars. Instead we go back to the times as much as the life; we try to picture the land and people that were the cradle of Burns's experience; and then we retrace the routes that link the poet with us today. What were the pressures, obstacles and influences that Burns faced? For better or worse, what caught the poet's imagination, what roused him to anger, what fooled him, what moved him? We are attempting to portray a man in his familiar – and to us unfamiliar – surroundings. A ready-made poet did not parachute to Earth with field rations of genius in his rucksack: his remarkable abilities were shaped by the world into which he was born, and in turn he had a hand in reshaping it.

Using *things* as evidence can open up new ways of seeing. One of the striking aspects of the past is how little survives physically. A simple test is to empty out your bag or pockets, or consider the clothes you stand in. In the hands of a good detective that would tell a lot about you. Yet how much will survive in twenty, let alone two hundred years? By that measure quite a lot connected with Burns has survived.

There are various ways of looking at these survivals. There is a certain

Agnes McLehose
(1759–1841) by John
Miers. Burns gave her
the the pen-name
'Clarinda'. Mrs
McLehose first
approached the poet
in December 1787,
curious to meet him.
She got more than she
bargained for.
Although she was
estranged from her
husband, as a genteel
married woman she
could not give way to
the attraction between
herself and Burns.
Burns relieved his
physical passion on
Nancy's servant lass,
Jenny Clow, and his
mental ardour in 'Ae
Fond Kiss'.

magic in pondering the original handwriting. You are following the movements of the same once-living hand that guided a plough, that raised a glass in a toast, that gripped the gauger's pistols, or that caressed a lover. But that kind of awareness is just a starting point that can lead us to other things. Take for instance the chair that fell off the cart when Burns was flitting from Mossgiel to Ellisland, and that he gave to the son of a neighbour who was standing nearby to give to his mother. It is a physical symbol of Burns's impulsive and generous nature. Clarinda's fantasy sketch of an imprisoned lady and her jailors has a disturbing undercurrent. This is the person who inspired 'Ae Fond Kiss', but what does it tell us, not just about Clarinda, but about the Burns who courted her good opinion? A fiddle made from the timber in Gavin Hamilton's office, where Robert and Jean formally married, is more than just an object in a zoo of relics. Would the man who made it not like to think that the music from the fiddle would take inspiration from the couple who once stood near it? This tells us something of the quality of the affection that Burns inspired in the folk memory.

To follow out the memory is as important as trying to figure out what life was like for Burns himself, because each generation has perceived Burns afresh, and that leads up to ourselves. Does that path end in a cardboard cut-out of Rhymer Rab? Is he among Edwin Muir's

> *… mummied housegods in their musty niches,*
> *Burns and Scott, sham bards of a sham nation …*
> SCOTLAND 1941

Or when we stop and consider, is his poetry and his memory altogether more formidable? Those small constellations of words that trip unthinkingly from our tongues – the best-laid schemes … to see oursels … a man's a man … ae fond kiss … a cup o' kindness … – where did they come from? And all the wisdom and humanity that they contain? It is curious to think that they came out of the remote westland muirs and ploughlands of an Ayrshire that had only just been touched by the Industrial Revolution, from a man who was often unwise and who died at thirty-seven, but who, as his friend Maria Riddell put it, had an irresistible attraction.

I inclose you a few lines I composed on a late melan-
choly occasion. — I will not give above five or six copies
of it at all, and I would be hurt if any friend should
give any copies without my consent. —

You cannot imagine, Clarinda, (I like the idea of Arcadian
names in a commerce of this kind) how much store
I have set by the hopes of your future friendship. —
I don't know if you have a just idea of my character, but I
wish you to see me—as I am. — I am, as most people of
my trade are, a strange will o' wisp being; the victim
too frequently of much imprudence and many follies. —
My great constituent elements are Pride and
Passion: the first I have endeavoured to humanize
into integrity and honour; the last makes me a
Devotee to the warmest degree of enthusiasm, in the
Love, Religion, & Friendship; either of them
or all together as I happen to be inspired. —
'Tis true, I never saw you but once; but how much
acquaintance did I form with you in that once!
Don't think I flatter you, or have a design upon

'My great constituent elements are Pride and Passion.' Robert Burns to Mrs Agnes McLehose, 28 December 1787.

NATIONAL LIBRARY OF SCOTLAND: ACC.9381/450

CHAPTER ONE

PORTRAITS

I don't know if you have a just idea of my character, but I wish you to see me as I am. — I am, as most people of my trade are, a strange will o' wisp being; the victim too frequently of much imprudence and many follies. — My great constituent elements are Pride and Passion: the first I have endeavoured to humanize into integrety and honour; the last makes me a Devotee to the warmest degree of enthusiasm, in Love, Religion, or Friendship …

That was how Robert Burns described himself to Nancy McLehose in a letter of 28 December 1787. As he wrote he was sitting in bed in a flat in Edinburgh's New Town, laid up with an injured knee, the result of a fall from a coach. He had met Mrs McLehose just over three weeks before and they had been instantly interested in one another. She was the same age as himself, estranged from her husband, and an evidently pretty woman. And it was she who had taken the initiative, inviting the poet to come and drink tea with her. It would have been one of his last social calls before he left Edinburgh to return to Ayrshire, but the accident intervened and he remained several weeks longer. From this relationship we are left with a famous exchange of letters between 'Sylvander' and 'Clarinda', as Burns now styled himself and Nancy, and that no less famous song of parting, 'Ae Fond Kiss'.

It is one of the peculiarities of human behaviour that we usually take others at their own valuation. We believe what people say about themselves until proven otherwise. Consider the boldness of the statement: 'a strange will o' wisp being … much imprudence and many follies … Pride and Passion … integrity and honour … Devotee … in Love, Religion, or

Friendship'. Was the poet's measure of himself true?

Burns mentioned two different things in his letter: marks of character he saw in himself, such as imprudence, and the stars by which he sought to steer his life, such as integrity; and in the middle, pride and passion. Burns both owned up to being proud and passionate, and valued pride and passion as qualities to aim for. Whichever direction and even erratic course he followed in life, he had these twin markers to steer by, and the internal compass that could find them.

But Burns's personal course came to an end two centuries ago. Can we ever *really* know what he was like? He swam in such a different sea, and if by some miracle we were to be plunged back into late eighteenth-century Scotland, we would find it as friendly as the surface of the planet Mars, so hostile was it to the many freedoms and comforts that we take for granted. On the other hand we might find values that we would want by some additional miracle to bring to our own age, such as open-handed hospitality, the ability to create social enjoyment out of virtually nothing, and a general intolerance of violence that we might find surprising. Even in thinking about it, we are often weighing up two things, balancing what we know of the constant old Adam in human nature against the moulding pressures of that different age.

This is the challenge of a portrait, especially one from another time. It is not just a physical likeness but a coded message that was open at the time of painting, but to understand it now we have to crack the code, break into systems, conventions and assumptions that are foreign to us and reconstruct them in our own imaginations. On the other hand there are so many casual images – as opposed to portraits – of Burns that tell us more about the people that made them than Burns himself. In unravelling all this we start where most portrait painters start, with the physical presence of the man himself and where he is positioned in the frame.

There was a time when most of the dead were buried in unmarked graves. Most old kirkyards are infinitely more crowded than the rows of headstones suggest. Digging a grave would usually produce a heap of bones from a previous generation, which would be placed in the ground again next to the new occupant. For most people it was just dust to dust, with the hope that, as in Montrose's words:

> *Lord (since Thou know'st where all these Atoms are)*
> *I'm hopeful, once Thou'lt recollect my Dust,*
> *And confident Thou'lt raise me with the Just.*

To have individuality perpetuated into earthly posterity was for a minority. And even that minority is always a shrinking one, the memorials fading under rain and frost, broken for building or drains, and in our own day destroyed to make car parks.

That fate escaped the gravestone of James Burnes and Margaret Falconer, his spouse, the poet's great grandparents, who died in 1745 and 1749 respectively. Theirs and another family headstone only survive today because they were restored in 1885, and additional protection from the weather placed over them at a later date. You can still see their headstones in Bervie kirkyard in Kincardineshire, the area that William Burnes, Burns's father, left for the south in 1748.

When William Burnes died, he also got a substantial headstone in Alloway kirkyard. Quarried away by souvenir hunters, it has twice been replaced in the original style. Agnes, who long survived her husband and famous son, is similarly interred with a gravestone along with other members of the family at Boulton, near Haddington, in East Lothian, in which district she and Robert's brother Gilbert and his family spent the latter parts of their lives.

The inscription on Burns's great grandfather's stone reads 'tenant in Brawliemuir'. To later generations that may seem unremarkable. At the time, like the headstone itself, it was a mark of status. As the laird held his land of the king, so the tenant held his land of the laird. But also, there were tenants and tenants. Before improved farming really spread outside the Lothians in the 1760s, many tenants were joint tenants. They might share their *tacks*, or leases, with several other tenants, and so the farm they rented would have a strong communal element. But the Burnes (or sometimes Burness) family were single tenants. They rented their lands from the Earl Marischal on the windy treeless braes of Glenbervie. Brawliemuir, Bogjorgan, Clochnahill: the names read like the frontier of a tribal territory. However, it was not to continue. As Gilbert Burns, Robert's younger brother recalled, 'I have often heard my father describe the anguish of mind he felt when he parted with his elder brother Robert on the top of a hill, on the confines of his native place, each going off his several way in search of new adventures, and scarcely knowing whither he went'. The reason for their departure was that Burns's grandfather, Robert Burnes, faced financial ruin. The combination of poor seasons and the economic disruption in that part of Scotland following the 1745 Jacobite rising had made it impossible to continue. But his son William never forgot that his family had been substantial tenant farmers. Later, once he had found his feet, his natural inclination was to re-establish himself in the same position as his forbears.

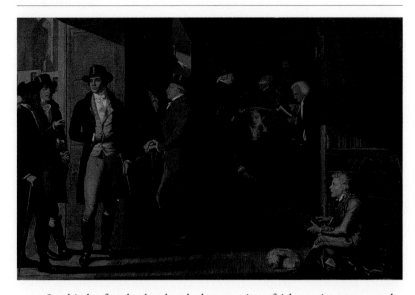

Robert Burns at Sibbald's Library by William Borthwick Johnstone. Painted half a century after the event, this shows the young Walter Scott staring at the great man as he enters the Lawnmarket shop. The painting is now displayed in The Writers' Museum, Lady Stair's Close, just off the Lawnmarket.

In this he faced a hard task, because in a fairly static economy the direction of social mobility is down. William Burnes would struggle – and succeed – to stay on the same level. This was not some kind of snobbery, but common sense. One major social divide at the time was between the gentry and the common people, but the common people still comprised the vast bulk of the population, and within that block there were huge differentials of both status and wealth – or more accurately, relative poverty. In the old pre-improvement farming (which we will consider below) tenants had their sub-tenants. When one considers that many of these tenants were joint tenants and themselves only small farmers, then the situation of their sub-tenants would hardly have been more than the barest of livings. They would labour to the tenants in return for a small scrap of land, a *yaird*, which was in effect a large garden on which they might raise a tiny crop or sustain a cow or one or two sheep. But the whole economic system was geared to having access to land, howsoever small that might be. What happened to those who through some misfortune such as a broken tenancy fell out of the system? There were precious few full-time alternatives in the countryside to farming. Country tradesmen such as smiths and *wrichts* or joiners, or *wabsters* or weavers, were also part-time farmers, as were estate officials. The full-time trades that existed in the small towns were jealously guarded by their practitioners. So beneath the farming population lay the nether reaches of almost unimaginable destitution. Yet as we shall see, people actually inhabited this region. The gap between these people and a substantial tenant farmer was vast.

In Burns's poetry we can pick out the representatives of people from every part of this spectrum, and he would champion all of them, 'the common people', yet most of them were in different circumstances and with very different expectations in life from himself. To posterity Burns would stand as a great tribune of the people. Indeed, he was, but like the original tribune he would be understanding and championing people who were much worse off than himself, or whose prospects in life were not just poor, but non-existent. Considering the hard life that the Burnes family faced at Mount Oliphant, this may seem strange, but it is fact. The converse is equally interesting. There is a thread in Burns's poetry (in 'The Twa Dogs' and 'The Jolly Beggars' for instance) where the poet recognises with a kind of respectful wonderment how, despite their harsh circumstances, the poorest of the poor could still enjoy themselves. What the poet saw and marvelled at was the triumph of the human spirit in appalling adversity.

We can place this man in his setting and say *what* he was — a farmer — but *who* he was is another matter. When we say that someone is 'always themselves', what part of the person are we thinking of? Like most people, Burns had various sides to his character that he revealed in different company. Once he was famous, the pressure on him to conform to other people's image of him was immense. When he arrived in Edinburgh among educated 'society', some were surprised when he did not turn out to be a rustic clown, others that he was not some simpering 'gentle shepherd' out of the pages of Allan Ramsay. On the other hand he had distinct peculiarities and minor eccentricities of dress and manner that marked him out in the country society of Ayrshire.

Burns inherited the image of the old-style independent farmer from his father William. The *guidman* was the patriarchal ruler of a farming household, who presided over the meals and prayers. That was the impression that Burns conveyed to the young Walter Scott when he saw him at Professor Ferguson's house at Sciennes in Edinburgh: 'I would have taken the poet, had I not known what he was, for a very sagacious country farmer of the old Scottish school; that is, none of your modern agriculturalists, who keep labourers for their drudgery, but the *douce guidman* who held his own plough'.

The nineteenth-century painting of Burns in Sibbald's Library in the Lawnmarket in Edinburgh, where Scott, the awe-struck laddie, gazes up at the great man as he enters, also catches something of this demeanour. In his riding boots Burns is quite distinct from the prominent urbanised gentlemen who surround him. He is well turned out (he always took care over his appearance), but still a countryman, a substantial farmer in his market clothes. Borthwick Johnston was of course following the style of clothes in which Burns was described. If Scott saw in Burns the manner of an old-fashioned farmer, he dressed as a modern successor, as a tenant farmer who might have ridden in from an improved farm in the Lothians.

Burns's portraits of the *guidman* are always vivid and never stereotyped. 'The Auld Farmer's New-Year Morning Salutation to his Auld Mare, Maggie' dwells reflectively on a sense of tradition, on a useful life well lived, a man at one with himself and his world:

> *Monie a sair darg we twa hae wrought,*
> *An wi the weary warl' fought!*
> *An monie an anxious day, I thought*
> *We wad be beat!*
> *Yet here to crazy Age we're brought,*
> *Wi something yet.*

Tam o' Shanter, also a *guidman*, based on Thomas Davidson, who farmed Shanter not far from Ayr, is an uncontrollable free spirit, a sociable rascal whose vices we secretly admire. The patriarch in 'The Cotter's Saturday Night', although in that setting a landless labourer, is in terms of personality a portrait of William, Burns's father.

> *The chearfu supper done, wi serious face,*
> *They, round the ingle, form a circle wide;*
> *The sire turns o'er, wi patriarchal grace,*
> *The big ha'-Bible, ance his father's pride.*
> *His bonnet rev'rently is laid aside,*
> *His lyart haffets wearing thin and bare;*
> *Those strains that once did sweet in Zion glide,*
> *He wales a portion with judicious care;*
> *And 'Let us worship God!' he says with solemn air.*

He stands for human dignity and spiritual values. In this trinity of the *guidman* we see Burns's unwitting portrait of himself.

One intriguing personal badge of identity that Burns created for himself was a version of armorial bearings. It may seem odd that the author of 'A man's a man' should indulge in such a pursuit. There was a practical point. Letters were not sent in envelopes, but the sheets themselves folded and sealed with a dod of wax that turned solid when it cooled, and so long

Dr John Moore
(1729–1802) by Sir
Thomas Lawrence. A
physician and
successful author,
Moore is only
remembered now
because in August
1787 Burns wrote to
him describing his
life hitherto. The
letter combines a
high-flown English
style with a certain
frankness and
valuable glimpses of
the poet's early years.

as the letter with the wax bearing the sender's unique mark of identity arrived unbroken, that proved that no one had tampered with the letter. For such a prolific letter-writer as Burns, some form of seal was natural. Yet in that age as well as this, arms were not an exclusive perquisite of the upper classes, and in his autobiographical letter to Dr John Moore of 2 August 1787 Burns made his own proud disclaimer of gentle descent: 'I have not the most distant pretensions to what the pyecoated guardians of escutcheons call, A Gentleman, – When at Edinburgh last winter, I got acquainted in the Herald's Office, and looking through that granary of Honors I there found almost every name in the kingdom; but for me,

" My ancient but ignoble blood
     Has crept thro' scoundrels ever since the flood"

Gules, Purpure, Argent, &c. quite disowned me'.

Incorporations of trades and not a few burgesses had arms. The gravestones of substantial *guidmen* often show the symbols of their calling – ox-yoke and the sock and coulter of a plough – set on a shield in a heraldic style. Burns described himself as something of a student of heraldry, and indeed acquired at least one book on the subject. Part of the attraction of arms is that they are a unique badge of personal and family identity. As Burns wrote to Alexander Cunningham, his Edinburgh lawyer friend, on 3 March 1794: 'I have invented one for myself [not quite: Maria Riddell helped him]; so, you know, I will be chief of the Name'. He then described his arms, which would include a holly bush, and a shepherd's pipe and crook. The crest was a woodlark perching on a sprig of bay-tree with the words 'Wood-notes wild', and at the bottom of the shield 'Better a wee bush than nae bield'. 'By the Shepherd's pipe & crook, I do not mean the nonsense of Painters of Arcadia; but a Stock-&-horn, & a Club; such as you see at the head of Allan Ramsay, in David Allan's quarto Edition of the Gentle Shepherd'. Here were the symbols by which Burns wished to be identified for posterity, a poet and *sangster* in the native tradition. There is no allusion to military prowess and grandeur, no 'helm befitting his degree'. This was added as a matter of form when, on the initiative of the Dumfries Burns Howff Club, the arms were matriculated in 1991.

Of course Burns was to have a final resting place infinitely grander than most. The irony of the grandeur of the mausoleum erected by public subscription to house his remains was not lost on observers such as Thomas Carlyle.

The significance of these marks of identity is the wish to be seen and remembered as an individual. This was a very human and earthly ambition, but not one that would find much favour with traditional Calvinistic Christianity; God in his heaven knew not just every individual but every hair on her or his head. All that mattered in this brief life was the destination of the soul, and any intervals of earthly enjoyment were snatched from between the travails of childbirth and the fangs of death. This focus on another world that one could neither see nor touch, yet which was assuredly there, and in the case of Hell terrifyingly real, produced a contempt and even hostility towards change in this world. This widely-held view affected quite practical matters. Colonel Ayton, writing *The Agriculture of Ayrshire* in 1811, remembered his youth when, rather than improve the soil and rid it of weeds, people were more taken up with church politics, and preferred 'to tread down the whore of Babylon and the Man of Sin'. Such was the hostility to change that when the Earl of Eglinton, who was keen on agricultural improvement, was murdered by a poacher, there was a general outcry that 'it was a punishment inflicted by heaven on the Earl for introducing innovations'.

In that context the notion of someone 'being himself' at all could be very difficult for anyone out of the ordinary. Individuals trying to change, to develop beyond the confines of their native heath, would be stigmatised. This has come down to modern Scotland in the sardonic expression: *'Ay, ay – I kent his faither'*, begging the question, why should he aspire to anything different? Burns did just that, and part of his strength to do it lay in this strong sense of self, what he was, where he came from and where he was going. As he said to his wife on his deathbed, 'Jean, a hundred years hence they will think more of me than they do now'. This was neither a wish nor a prayer, but what he knew to be fact. But for that reason, it is of some fascination to see the man as others saw him at the time.

There were several portraits painted of Burns. The first, by Peter Taylor, a coach-painter to trade, was said by Mrs McLehose and Sir Walter Scott to be a good likeness. Nevertheless, it shows a different face from the others. Most famous is Alexander Nasmyth's head and shoulders. This was to be the basis of an engraving to go in the Edinburgh edition of the poems. John Beugo worked from it to produce the engraving, but he also had several sittings with Burns to keep him on the right track. Some at the time thought it a better likeness than Nasmyth's portrait. It is harder and less romantic than the painting, and conveys more of Burns's formidable intellect.

Early one fine morning Burns and Nasmyth (who became a close friend) walked out from Edinburgh to Roslin, and there the artist stole a sketch while the poet was contemplating the beauty of the scene. This formed

Robert Burns by
Alexander Reid.
Watercolour on ivory,
c. 1795–6.

the basis of the later full-length portrait. Alexander Reid painted a miniature in Dumfries the year before Burns died, and Burns himself thought it a good likeness. It is clearly an older and more mature face. Burns was increasingly suffering from the illness that would carry him away, and perhaps this accounts for the more distant impression that it conveys.

There were two other portraits that were derived from the Nasmyth head and shoulders. One was almost a caricature of the poet as one of the figures in David Allan's illustration of 'The Cotter's Saturday Night'. Burns is shown as the eldest son at his father's side. The other was a chalk drawing by Alexander Skirving done a year after the poet's death. It has a fineness of detail absent in the others, and shows the 'massiveness' of the head that people remarked upon at the time. The most striking feature is the alert penetrating eye. Perhaps this is what led Sir Walter Scott to pronounce it 'the only good portrait of Burns'.

Scott was a lad of fifteen when Burns came to Edinburgh. Besides seeing the poet in the street, he was present at a gathering at Professor Ferguson's house in Sciennes where Burns was the principal guest. Scott recalled that it was the poet's eye that was remarkable: 'It was large, and of a dark cast, and glowed (I say literally *glowed*) when he spoke with feeling or interest. I never saw such another eye in a human head'. Others noted the same. Josiah Walker, an educationalist who published a *Life of Burns* in 1811, recalled that 'in his large dark eye the most striking index of his genius resided. It was full of mind'. Generally people were unfailingly struck by the mobility and expressiveness of Burns's features. But as Maria Riddell recalled, 'his voice alone could improve on the magic of his eye; sonorous, replete with the finest modulations'.

Burns's hair was black and thin and he usually tied it in a *queue* or tail. In Tarbolton parish he was the only man to do so, although neither there nor in Edinburgh did he powder it, as was fashionable at the time. His complexion was dark, and its roughness marked him as one who had toiled in sun, rain and wind. The fact that he had been doing a man's work almost from the age of thirteen had also taken its toll, and he had a decided ploughman's stoop. Josiah Walker noticed that 'his stature, from want of setting up, appeared to be only of the middle size, but was rather above it'.

Indeed, Burns's manner always struck cultivated people as that of a countryman, but it was never awkward or clownish. 'Manly' is a frequent description, and it conveyed something of his character that fascinated them. Scott defined it as 'a sort of dignified plainness and simplicity, which received part of its effect perhaps from one's knowledge of his extraordinary talents'.

Many of the eye-witness accounts of Burns relate to his visits to Edinburgh, and they all concur in his sure-footed demeanour and self-confidence. Robert Anderson was a literary figure who would produce *A Complete Edition of the Poets of Great Britain* between 1792 and 1795. It was on account of his literary interests that he was invited to meet Burns. He first saw him in the house of David Ramsay, printer of the newspaper the *Edinburgh Courant*: 'In the midst of a large company of ladies and gentlemen assembled to see him, and attentive to his every look, word and motion, he was in no way disconcerted, but seemed perfectly easy, unembarrassed and unassuming'. For many this was quite at odds from what they expected of 'an uneducated rustic'. In fact several people remarked that his conversation was even more fascinating than his poetry. Dugald Stewart was professor of moral philosophy at Edinburgh University. He had already met Burns in Ayrshire, and was to show the poet kindness and hospitality in Edinburgh. He noted 'the fluency, and precision, and originality of his language'. In the polite society that was then attempting to master spoken English, Burns actually had a better grasp of it than most. The only hint of affectation that Stewart noted was the poet introducing occasionally a word or phrase in French. He doubted if Burns had more than a smattering of it, although in fact Burns had a reasonable reading knowledge of the language.

Robert Burns by Archibald Skirving. Chalk, *c.* 1796–8.
SCOTTISH NATIONAL PORTRAIT GALLERY

The accounts of Burns's conversation differ in emphasis. In a society where style and manner were of the utmost importance, those of a more conventional mould were nervous of the poet's directness, mistaking it for uneducated dogmatism, and imputed it to what Josiah Walker thought was 'his inexperience in those modes of smoothing dissent and softening assertion, which are important characteristics of polished manners'. Those of larger intellect perceived Burns differently. Dugald Stewart recalled that 'he took his share in conversation, but not more than belonged to him; and listened with apparent attention and deference, on subjects where his want of education deprived him of the means of information'. Scott agreed: 'Among the men who were the most learned of their time and country, he expressed himself with perfect fitness, but without the least intrusive forwardness'.

Robert Burns by Alexander Nasmyth. Pencil, undated.
SCOTTISH NATIONAL PORTRAIT GALLERY

The way Burns dressed – then as now an important social signal – generally struck people as being of a piece with the man, 'plain and unpretending, with a sufficient attention

to neatness', according to Dugald Stewart. It struck most as 'being that of a farmer of the better sort', with his 'dark coloured coat, light figured waistcoat, shirt with ruffles at the breast and boots in which he constantly visited and walked about town'. The boots caught more than one person's eye. He always wore them, and, on special occasions, a pair of buckskin breeches.

Not a few illustrators have mistakenly portrayed Burns at the plough thus. The reality there was different. William Clark, who was *fee'd* or hired at Ellisland for the Martinmas term in 1789, recalled Burns's dress at home, with his broad, blue bonnet, long-tailed coat, corduroy breeches, dark-blue stockings, the *cootikens* or anklets that stopped the *gutters* or mud and stones from getting into his shoes as he worked, and, in the cold weather, the black-and-white checked plaid. This is the picture that was never painted from life.

Direct eye-witness descriptions of Burns as a native of Ayrshire and a working farmer are not so common, yet even the scraps give an interesting portrait. It is the same person but with a different emphasis: the man who could captivate the capital's society with his conversation could 'set the rustic circle in a roar'.

Burns was noticed early as different, not just because he tied his hair, but because he wore his plaid to the kirk. He had what were perceived to be eccentricities that related directly to his literary and poetic preoccupations. He was noted to be an insatiable reader, to the point that he read even through meal-times, so absorbed that the spoon might fall from his hand. John Lambie, who was *fee'd* at Mossgiel, recalled that Burns could be a dangerous man to thresh with. This was done with the flail – 'the weary flingin tree' – often by two people working on opposite sides of the sheaves, striking turn about. Burns would sometimes be working to the rhythm of the tunes or lines in his head, and when these changed, so would his pace, to the considerable danger of his partner. Out in the fields his preoccupation amused the other workers and drove his brother Gilbert to distraction, as carts of manure stood unloaded while a poem was forming in his head. Or he would work without conversing, his lips moving silently. Often it was the farm servants who kept Burns right in the work.

Both John Lambie at Mossgiel and Willie Clark at Ellisland remembered Burns as a kind, and indeed indulgent, master. His temperament was generally easy-going, but on occasion he could flare into a rage that sent the servants bolting for cover. One such event was when a servant lass had chopped the potatoes too big and there was a danger of the cattle choking on them. Yet Burns's temper would cool as quickly as it had arisen. On one occasion in Edinburgh he was spied in a great rage on his way to thrash the

Opposite:
Robert Burns by
Alexander Nasmyth.
Oil on panel, 1828.

SCOTTISH NATIONAL PORTRAIT
GALLERY

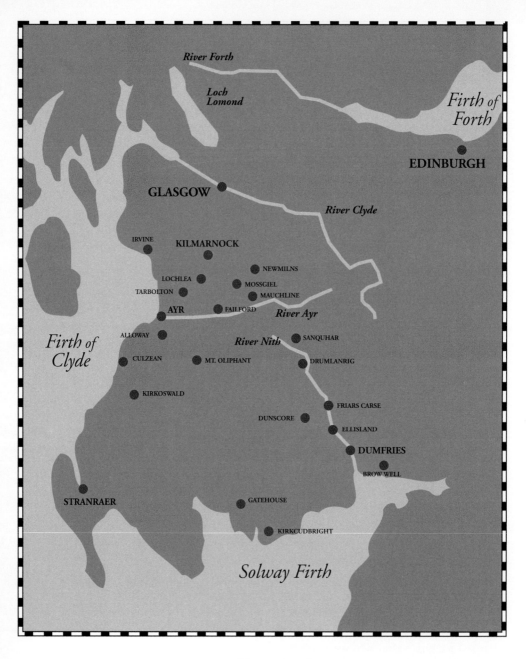

Map of 'Burns Country'.

publisher William Creech to get the money long owed him. Before Burns found him, his temper had cooled to something much more deadly:

> *A little upright, pert, tart, tripping wight,*
> *And still his precious Self his dear delight;*
> *Who loves his own smart shadow in the streets*
> *Better than e're the fairest She he meets.*
>
> LETTER TO MRS DUNLOP OF DUNLOP

Once Burns had conceived a dislike for someone, it was just a matter of time before this would be vented in verse that would be laced with not the kindest of wit, especially if his pride had been damaged. That pride, as we shall see, was an ill thing to meddle with.

Although at Ellisland Burns and his family ate separately from the servants, he always treated them with familiarity, and equally important, he saw that they were duly paid; Jean also saw that they were well fed. As his work with the Excise grew, it drew him away from farm work, but that did not prevent him from working at the plough from time to time, and making a good job of it. At seed-time Burns would be out in the parks early in the morning with his sowing sheet. It was not a job that he particularly relished, which is not surprising, as hand sowing is not a natural motion.

> *Forjesket sair, with weary legs,*
> *Rattlin the corn out-owre the rigs*
>
> SECOND EPISTLE TO J. LAPRAIK

The point may have been a habitual carefulness against waste, common to country people. Bad ploughing that left open seams and careless sowing was an easy way to waste grain, so Burns saw to it himself where he could. Gilbert Burns, who kept the accounts at Mossgiel, noted that his brother was careful with money, and never lived beyond the tight limits that the family had set itself.

When there was extra work, Burns would sometimes produce a dram, but not always. Nor did Willie Clark ever see Burns drunk in his six months there. Likewise, Gilbert Burns noted that he never saw his brother affected by drink until he was thrown into wider company when his fame grew. It may have taken very little to affect him, for Burns himself mentioned to Dugald Stewart that his habitual sobriety was not from virtuous choice, for too much did not agree with his stomach. Paradoxically, for the man

The young Walter Scott meets Burns in Dr Adam Ferguson's house at Sciennes in Edinburgh. This was painted by Charles Martin Hardie a century after the event, working from original portraits of the participants. The house still stands, incorporated into the surrounding tenements. Scott was the only person in a distinguished company who could identify the quotation under a painting that had caught Burns's eye.

MRS PATRICIA MAXWELL-SCOTT, ABBOTSFORD

who extolled the virtues of whisky in verse, Burns did not seem to have any overriding interest in drink itself, for the occasions when he drank alone appear to have been rare. David Sillar, the 'Davie' of the two Epistles, was a teacher in Tarbolton. He remembered that 'we frequently met upon Sundays at church, when between sermons [ie between services], instead of going with our friends or lasses to the inn, we often took a walk in the fields'. There are other instances when Burns turned down the chance of a drink for a walk.

However, one thing that Davie Sillar noted, and wryly envied, was his friend's ease with women: 'In these walks I have frequently been struck by his facility in addressing the fair sex: and many times when I have been bashfully anxious how to express myself, he would have entered into a conversation with them with the greatest of freedom'. It was not always so. Gilbert Burns remembered that at first the young Robert was bashful and awkward with women. Only when he approached manhood did 'his attachment to their society become very strong, and he was constantly the victim of some fair enslaver'. Gilbert thought that Robert's imagination often supplied the qualities of attraction that were wanting in reality. Whether this was indeed true, or whether it was that the poet's eye could see qualities to which his more cautious brother was blind, we will never know. As we shall see, there were other female characteristics that were just as important to Burns as physical appearance.

Animals were also a matter of great concern to him. Burns was evidently careful of his livestock's welfare, and had a particularly soft spot for his pet sheep at Ellisland. In his feeling for the brute creation he often held up a mirror to himself, as in 'To a Mouse'.

His love of animals did not extend to lice, yet one such provided the occasion for that famous reflection that he must often have applied to himself:

> O wad some Power the giftie gie us
> To see oursels as ithers see us!
> It wad frae monie a blunder free us
> An foolish notion …
>
> TO A LOUSE

Yet Burns did not always heed how others saw him, and that is a blessing, otherwise, with all his qualities and faults and follies and glories, he would not have been the man he was.

CHAPTER TWO

ORIGINAL BURNS COUNTRY

The painful parting that William Burnes described took place in 1748. William's eldest brother James had already settled in Montrose, where his branch of the family would prosper. It was Robert and William who left for the south to try their luck. Robert went to Ayrshire, where he worked in a lime quarry and later set up a small school for farmers' sons. Robert Burnes was never a fit man, and when he died in 1789 his namesake poet nephew showed great kindness to his family. William, the youngest, went to Edinburgh, where he got work as a landscape gardener. There he probably met Alexander Fairlie of Fairlie, an Ayrshire laird, and in 1750 he headed south west to work as his gardener. Translated into modern terms, this would have been a semi-professional job. The laird's relationship with his gardener was a direct and personal one. The gardener would shape the *policies,* or the landscape, that lay about the *big houss,* or the laird's seat. The vegetables and fruit that came to the laird's table, which he might on occasion send to his neighbours as presents, were the result of his gardener's skill. However, Fairlie was no ordinary laird. He was an energetic enthusiast of what was then known as 'improvement' – in effect the start of the Agricultural Revolution. This had already taken root in the Lothians, but in Ayrshire it was just beginning, and Fairlie was one of the prime movers. He not only applied improvement to his own ground, but as *factor* or executive manager to the Eglinton estates he set this going on one of the biggest blocks of landholding in Ayrshire. Personal contact with this man must have been an important factor in William's later efforts to return to his family's situation as tenant farmers – with the one difference: that they would be 'improving' farmers.

Nevertheless, William's emotional and spiritual roots ran back into the old Scotland. He was a deeply religious patriarch of his family, and was cautious of the greater personal freedoms that were emerging at the time. This zeal for improvement and education, combined with an emotionally conservative temperament, was part of the age, an ambivalent set of mind that he seems to have passed on to his sons.

William moved on from Fairlie to set out the policies at Doonside, near Alloway. Alloway was a small wayside village on the road south from Ayr to Maybole. He must have prospered in his gardening enterprises, for there he bought seven and a half acres of ground. This he called 'New Gardens', with the intention of starting his own nursery garden as an extension of his landscaping work. William also started building a house. In 1756 he had met Agnes Brown, the daughter of Gilbert Brown, a substantial tenant farmer in Craigenton, near Kirkoswald. Agnes was a small, neat and sturdily-built woman with pale red hair, and, as her daughter Isabel recalled, with 'dark eyes often ablaze with a temper difficult to control', but overall with an easy-going and cheerful temperament and a fund of good common sense. This was the person William took back to Alloway as his bride after they were married on 15 December 1757. In the event, New Gardens never came to anything as a nursery. The practical Agnes put cows on the ground and started a small cheese-making business. Just over a year after she was married she gave birth to Robert Burns.

This birth was marked by a drastic domestic upturn. The fireplace had been built more solidly than the flanking walls, so that parts of the gable settled at different rates. The added stress of a storm caused a partial collapse. Agnes and the infant Robert were forced to vacate the bed – still there to be seen – and seek shelter with a neighbour.

> *'Twas then a blast o Janwar win'*
> *Blew hansel in on Robin.*
> THERE WAS A LAD

The building is symbolic of more than the birthplace of a great poet. It probably reached its present form after several years of occupancy by the Burns family. (Other later additions have been demolished.) To start with, it would have consisted of the living room and a byre next to it, divided off

Robert Burns's Cottage at Alloway by Sam Bough. Painted over a century after William Burnes built the cottage, this shows the pub extension at the end (since demolished), and the extensively re-built walls and lum-heads. Bough knew his Burns, and must have relished his descriptions of winter.

GLASGOW MUSEUMS & ART GALLERIES

by the bed and *hallan,* or partition. Then the existing combined byre and stable would have been built, the old byre becoming a general store-room and milk-house, with perhaps additional box-beds for the growing family. After that the present barn would have been built. Originally the floor of the living quarters would have been clay, and the fire, one burning peats, would have been on floor level. The second fireplace in the building dates from later last century, and may have replaced an earlier one.

In its general shape the house at Alloway follows an ancient pattern that can be seen in neighbouring countries in North West Europe – the long house with dwelling, byre and other parts built in line, all with internal communication. There is still the occasional house in Lowland Scotland today where one can sit in comfort by the fire in the living room and hear the rustle and movement of the beasts through the door in the adjoining byre, and smell their sweat and muck and feel their warmth, and know that in fact it is not unpleasant, and a profoundly striking link with the past.

The house in Alloway has long been identified as the *auld clay biggin* or old clay building of a vanished age. The impression is that even in Burns's youth it represented something old. That is true of the pattern, but many

28

of the features bore the stamp of novelty. Indeed, it is possible to imagine that on the collapse of the gable the neighbours would have shaken their heads and wondered why William Burnes had not stuck to the old methods of construction: erecting a framework of *couples* or wooden crucks, and filling in the walls and gables with field-stone bedded in *fail* or sods. Instead of building a new-fangled flue into the thickness of the gable, he could have just put up a *hingin lum* or simple funnel, of timber and clay, against the inside of the gable to carry up the smoke. They might have surmised that William Burnes was experimenting with *fantoush* or fanciful notions of modernity that he had picked up in his travels, and which he was now inflicting on himself and his family.

In fact early last century considerable sections of the walls had to be rebuilt because William's idiosyncratic roof construction had forced the wallheads outwards and destroyed them. By that time the building had become a wayside inn, no doubt trading on its fame as the poet's birthplace. Had it not been for this, all trace of the house that William Burnes built would have vanished, and no one would have given his handiwork a second thought.

Thus the house at Alloway is a true symbol of the times that Robert was born into. Change there has always been, but during the poet's thirty-seven years, the countryside, which was the backdrop to most of his experience, was changing with unprecedented rapidity. During precisely that period the first stage of the Agricultural Revolution was roaring through Lowland Scotland, changing the economic and social order and challenging old values. As a working farmer, Robert Burns would have encountered these changes on a daily basis.

'The Cotter's Saturday Night' is set in the house of a landless labourer. Such was the effect of the poem that it became a favourite for illustration. It is difficult to distinguish what was dictated by an idealistic attraction to the event being portrayed, what they chose to see, and what they did not or would not or even could not notice, because the artists were for the most part from a different social background. There are other rare pictures from the same era which merely show interiors without relation to any event. One such is Alexander Carse's *Evening in a Scots Cottage*. There is nothing remarkable about the characters or scene except that it shows a whole complex of life that Burns himself knew was vanishing. This we know, because the little group of people are whiling away the hours of darkness in listening to a man playing the stock-and-horn. A laddie also has another stock-

Evening in a Scots Cottage by Alexander Carse. Although the cottage at Alloway was more comfortable than this, the blend of a bleak setting and absorbing company would have been familiar to Burns. Burns used the stock-and-horn as a symbol in his seal, although it is not certain he ever heard one played. It would have sounded like a rough version of a chanter.

NATIONAL GALLERY OF SCOTLAND

and-horn in his hands, and he is watching and learning the fingering of the player. There are now only three of these old instruments known to exist, all of them probably made as a record of a passing curiosity. The stock-and-horn was a simple woodwind instrument in which the player blew into a reed, and in Burns's day it was apparently disused, driven out by more highly developed pipes, or the brilliant and versatile fiddle.

There are numerous other features in Carse's picture that would continue much longer, yet even at that period they were old fashioned. A *cruisie* lamp hangs above the fire, and the man drinks his ale from a wooden *coggie*. That ale would not have been the brewster's or victualler's *nappy* of the inn, but the weak and malty produce made at home, which was the easiest way of getting nutrition from the crop of *bere* or barley. The only chair in the house is occupied by the father of the household, the rest sit on *creepies* or simple wooden stools. Sticks rather than peats burn on the fire. Perhaps that is to give more light, or maybe the family is not well enough placed to have right of access to a peat-moss. The single most valuable thing to be seen is the iron pot over the fire, and the links that support it. The rest is bare and spartan – clay floor, rough-hewn timber, the roof open to the underside of the thatch, and a drab curtain to conceal the box-bed in the wall.

Carse's picture shows something old fashioned rather than physically old. Such houses were reared out of the land that they stood in, and to that they would return. Much of the fabric was part of the organic cycle of farming. Old thatch and the sod component of the walls would end up on the *midden* with the muck from the byre, ash from the fire and even dead dogs, cats and vermin, this mass of putrefaction going back to *guid* or fertilise the land. Often people owned their own cruck-frames, and when they *flittit* or moved house they could be uprooted and, like clumsy tent frames, planted elsewhere until even they crumbled under the processes of nature. Acts of the old Parliament refer to *the puir pepilis, the inhabitaris of the grund*. That vivid phrase conveys much.

These *inhabitaris of the grund* were the cotters. They had other names also, such as *grassmen* or *acremen*, and would become a vanished race. They were often the sub-tenants referred to earlier. Their sons and daughters would also try to get live-in jobs as servants to tenant farmers. In Burns's day they were making the transition from sub-tenants to *fairm sairvants* – wholly paid employees with no land.

Before improvement, the people they worked for, the tenants proper, lived in houses that were built on the same lines of construction, but more elaborately, with a *ben* or inner room reached through the main living space. This ben room was in Ayrshire known as the *spence*, private to the *guidman* or farmer and the *guidwife*. In that society to have such domestic privacy was a great luxury, but one which despite the smoky fire and vermin in the thatch Burns re-created in 'The Vision':

> *And when the day had clos'd his e'e*
> *Far i the west,*
> *Ben i the spence, right pensivelie,*
> *I gaed to rest.*

Here Burns was casting his mind back to a setting that his family had left behind by the time he wrote 'The Vision', but it was a scene that he obviously knew. Part of Burns's immediate appeal among the Ayrshire country people was the novel way in which he conveyed a sense of personal, and indeed private, experience, because the common people saw little enough of privacy. The youngest children in a better tenant's house might sleep in the *spence* with their parents, but generally life in these old houses was lived in public. The servants would sleep on *settils* or long seats and benches in the main living part of the house, or perhaps the half-loft above it, if there was one; the boys and men would sometimes sleep over the horses in the stable. People dressed and undressed in front of one another; they ate together

Fragment of William Burnes's farm account book from the early 1770s. The
entry 'To a hoe mended' was written by Robert Burns when he was about
fourteen, and is believed to be the earliest known example of his handwriting.
NATIONAL LIBRARY OF SCOTLAND: MS.586.

and they prayed together. It was this communal way of life that fascinated the genre painters of the early nineteenth century in particular, and because they were travelling fast away from it, they wished to reflect not just an interesting scene, but people who could be poor and civilised at the same time.

Before improvement, people were thus tied to *the grund* as well as to any master or over-tenant. They were also tied to the landscape in another way: by a total reliance on its natural resources that ran much further than the fabric of the houses.

As with the housing, this old landscape requires some considerable effort to re-create in our imaginations, because it would appear staggeringly different to us. If the houses would have looked ramshackle and untidy to our eye, so would the land. Today, even in remote parts of the hills, we can see defining dry-stane dykes that run like zippers, dividing one part from another. In the old landscape it would have been impossible to discern even the suggestion of one straight line. Field shapes, tracks, yards, houses, all would have had a totally irregular configuration. The lines of definition would have been unfamiliar in other ways. The privacy of property was not important, but possession was, and to possess certain rights in land was a concept as important as ownership, because possession through a *holding* or tenancy was what gave access to a vital range of natural resources that were held *in commonty* or commonly. This included fuel, timber and pasture. The fuel was of obvious importance, because without it for cooking or comfort there could be no sustained settlement. The timber – what there was of it – was vital for the houses and implements. The pasture included most of the land. *Commonty* did not mean a free-for-all, in fact quite the reverse. It required a discipline of fair shares that stopped waste, and barred those who were outside the community from raiding these precious resources.

This meant that the land was used in a quite different way. The main pasture was separate from the ploughed land, and was not the sward of luxuriant, cultivated grass that is common today. One commonly used word for pasture was *muir*, or, as it is still often pronounced in the country today, *mair*. To the modern ear this implies something approaching wasteland, fit only for wildfowl and a very thin scatter of sheep. In Burns's childhood, *muir* was where most of the livestock grazed outside the winter months. Before improvement broke up this old pattern, most of the land in Ayrshire was rough grazing. If that seems strange, there are places in Denmark and the Netherlands where a similar landscape is still within living memory,

Arbroath in the
1690s, from John
Slezer's *Theatrum
Scotiae*. William
Burnes's homeland
was a little to the
north. These snaking
rigs or ploughed-up
ridges helped
drainage. In Burns's
day they were being
straightened and
fenced with hedges
and drystane dykes
as part of the
Agricultural
Revolution.

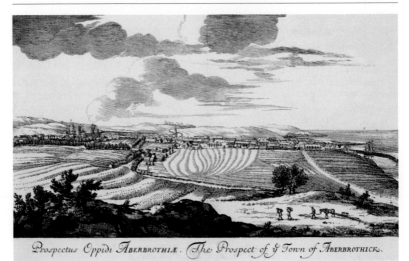

Prospectus Oppidi Aberbrothiæ. The Prospect of ye Town of Aberbrothick.

and now they struggle to preserve the last scraps of *heide* or *moer* for posterity. Burns's joking reference to 'some muirlan' tip' (a ram roaming over the common grazing) hints at some rough old freedom. The romance of the Gentle Shepherd lay not in some sunny pastorale of a Mediterranean landscape, but the freedom of windy hillsides and the *beild* or sheltered spots by the banks of waters that cut through land that had never seen a plough. It was a rough, open landscape sporting a wide range of wild grasses, heather, sedges and *rashes* or rushes.

The in-by land, in Ayrshire commonly the *croft* land, was always under crop. Land on the margins, the *outfield*, was cropped from time to time until the yield did not repay the effort, but was mostly a reserve of grazing and a quarry for the *fail* or sods widely used for building and so on. Cultivated land was laid out in *rigs* or ridges, a feature which appears in Burns's poetry. The means of cultivation had been changing before Burns's day. Both horses and oxen – or more generally cattle – were used for ploughing, but in Burns's Ayrshire the latter were becoming a memory. Not just ploughing but the animals themselves featured vividly in his imagination. In 'The Cotter's Saturday Night' there are 'the miry beasts retreating frae the pleugh'. In the 'Auld Farmer's New-Year Morning Salutation to his Auld Mare':

> *Thou was a noble fittie-lan',*
> *As e'er in tug or tow was drawn!*
> *Aft thee an' I, in aught hours' gaun,*
> *On guid March-weather,*

Hae turn'd sax rood beside our han',
For days thegither.

Of course, the relationship between man and beast was much more than sentiment, it was one of total interdependence. It was the livestock that provided the vital link between the *muir* and the *croft* land. The animals' muck converted the lower grade potential of one and concentrated it on the other, thus making it possible to keep on cropping the ploughed land continuously, as we still crop vegetable gardens today. Animals were the medium between people and the land, not a crop to be consumed. People lived through the animals' products of milk, eggs, wool and strength in the plough. They were only killed if there was no prospect of being able to keep them through the winter, when they would become a wasting asset. Otherwise animals would only be consumed direct if they died of disease, such as a *braxy* sheep, or on a special occasion such as a wedding. This more archaic involvement with animals is one which must have informed Burns's attitude directly.

Then there was the *hairst* or harvest. This was the most exciting and fraught time of the year. There was the race to get the crop safely in before it might get destroyed by the boisterous equinoctial weather, and then the high point of release when that labour was over, and the *corn-yaird* was, hopefully, full of fat *rucks* or stacks roped and thatched against the worst of winter. The *hairst* demanded every spare hand available, and the strain of the work would wrinkle out every peculiarity of human behaviour. As Burns recalled in his verse epistle to Elizabeth Scott in 'To the Guidwife of Wauchope House:'

> *When first amang the yellow corn*
> *A man I reckon'd was,*
> *An wi the lave ilk merry morn*
> *Could rank my rig and lass:*
> *Still shearing, and clearing*
> *The tither stookèd raw,*
> *Wi clavers and havers,*
> *Wearing the day awa.*

More specifically, it was the start of many a courtship, as in Ayrshire it was the custom to pair a young woman and man to shear together, as Burns described his encounter with 'Handsome Nell' in the same poem:

The Hairst Rig from
P. Hately Waddell's
*Life and Works of
Robert Burns*
(Glasgow, 1867).
Gathering a harvest
using only hand tools
was a laborious task,
but the *hairst* was
also, as Burns fondly
recorded, the scene of
much conviviality,
and many a youthful
tryst.

NATIONAL LIBRARY OF
SCOTLAND

*I see her yet, the sonsie quean
That lighted up my jingle,
Her witching smile, her pauky een
That gart my heart-strings tingle!*

This could be turned on its head in a wonderful nonsense jingle:

*Robin shure in hairst,
I shure wi him:
Fient a heuk had I,
Yet I stack by him.*

ROBIN SHURE IN HAIRST

The Ayrshire countryside of the poet's youth – at least in his mind's
eye – was an integrated whole that was stocked and cropped and peopled.
That may explain Burns's total lack of interest in the sea, which may have
appeared a desert in comparison. His vision in the opening verse of 'The

Holy Fair' alludes to all the elements of pasture, crops and the wild life, and also, with the reference to the day of rest and worship, to belief. Furthermore, he, too, is also part of the scene:

> Upon a simmer Sunday morn,
> When Nature's face is fair,
> I walkèd forth to view the corn,
> An snuff the caller air.
> The rising sun, owre Galston Muirs
> Wi glorious light was glintin;
> The hares were hirplin down the furs,
> The lav'rocks they were chantin
> Fu sweet that day.

This kind of integration, the sense of one world, would have seemed natural in the old pre-improvement society. It was dominated by *neibourin*, or communal activity. For even the most recalcitrant, some dour co-operation would have been conscripted. Much of the work around activities such as the harvest, herding and handling livestock, the winning of fuel and the building of houses involved neighbouring. The ploughing, commonly with four horses, could mean neighbours combining to make a team. The necessity for co-operation would also have brought its portion of bickering, rows and fearsome *faa-outs* over who was due what. Formerly there had

Mount Oliphant, Ayrshire, sketched by W. L. Leitch *c.* 1827–30. In these early Ayrshire 'improved' buildings the house was set at right-angles to the byre, stable and cart-shed. Burns repeated this pattern in the buildings at Ellisland in Dumfriesshire. Reproduced from the *Burns Chronicle and Club Directory* (Kilmarnock, 1932).
NATIONAL LIBRARY OF SCOTLAND

been a focus for the organisation of communal activities in the Baron Court. If people were sneaking more than their fair share of livestock on to the *commonty* or taking more peat or timber than was their due, it would be settled in open court under the eye of the *baron baillie*, the laird's depute, or perhaps even *himself*. These organisations had been falling into disuse, and just before Burns's time they were severely curtailed in the Heritable Jurisdictions Act of 1747, part of the break-up of the old system that was proceeding apace.

In parallel with the communal ethos, it was also a hard world of do-it-yourself and self-help. The degree of specialisation was low, and, as we will see, the few tradesmen were usually part-time farmers. In general, people had to know not only how to farm; they also had to build and thatch their houses, make and mend their own implements and harness, find their own fuel, produce their own spun yarn for the weaver, know how to process and preserve all the animal products. The knowledge required to cope with ailments in animals or people all depended on inherited experience. A sudden death could deprive people of, for example, a smith who knew about lameness in animals or a *howdie* or midwife who could negotiate the dangers of childbirth, and there might be no easy replacement. All these things had to be solved or suffered locally.

One countervailing advantage then was that people of outstanding ability were not automatically draughted out of the community through the conduit of a meritocratic education system. To a remarkable degree the tie of the land has retained the yeast of sharp intelligence in the country populations of Scotland today. In Burns's time, that would have been so commonplace as to be unremarkable.

But the community, this hierarchy of lairds, tenants and their sub-tenants had little means of coping with what Luath in 'The Twa Dogs' called 'want o' maisters', and what we would now describe as unemployment. In a society where public expenditure was virtually nil, and where people attended to most of their own needs, there was little opportunity for those who had fallen out of the system to make a living. Even the wandering *packman* with his poke of threads and needles and other odds and ends needed a modest capital. Destitution was a constant social problem, a terrifying sump which lay just beneath the web of mutual debt that pervaded much of eighteenth-century Scotland. There were various ways in which society attempted to cope with it. Every parish collected for the poor, and this *aliment* was distributed among the aged and infirm. An honest and perhaps older person who had fallen on hard times might get a licence to beg. That was common enough to make a joke of it:

Mossgiel, watercolour by J. Kennedy. Here the steadings have been extended since Burns's day and the trees have matured, but the house is still of one storey, setting the scene at about 1850.

NATIONAL GALLERY OF SCOTLAND

Auld age ne'er mind a feg;
The last o't, the warst o't,
Is only but to beg.

EPISTLE TO DAVIE

Sir Walter Scott painted a vivid picture of a licensed beggar in Eddie Ochiltree in *The Antiquary*. Beyond that were the *sturdy beggars*, able-bodied people who were numerous enough to form a sub-culture of their own, and who were seen as preying on the settled population and a law unto themselves. For them there was no solution. Where the kirk sessions had the power, they harried those they contemptuously called *sorners* – 'spongers' is the nearest English equivalent – out of the district to inflict themselves elsewhere. Even here Burns was ambivalent. By definition, 'honest poverty' implied that there was another sort. Yet he could sympathise with the condition of those 'randy gangrel bodies' that he describes in 'The Jolly Beggars'. As the disabled soldier sings:

And now, tho I must beg, with a wooden arm and leg,
And many a tatter'd rag hanging over my bum,
I'm as happy with my wallet, my bottle and my callet,
As when I us'd in scarlet to follow a drum.

39

In destitution lay a kind of grim liberty, and Burns had the sympathetic insight to see that if that was your lot, you might as well get drunk and enjoy it.

A place where the 'Jolly Beggars' got drunk was Poosie Nancy's *howff* in Mauchline, a dosshouse that catered for such social flotsam. Mauchline has a history that goes back to the mid-fourteenth century when Walter the Steward, King Robert the Bruce's son-in-law, gave the lands of 'the plain with the pool' to Melrose Abbey. There is a significance in that meaning, for, as with the name Mossgiel itself (*moss* being a peat-bog), it was then the kind of place that Cistercian monks liked: remote, undeveloped and not particularly inviting. But by 1315 the district was recognised as a parish, and in 1510 it was raised into a Burgh of Regality with a weekly market and an annual fair. To modern eyes it would have seemed a village.

The Burghs included a core of old foundations that went back much further than Mauchline, mostly the much grander Royal Burghs that had a monopoly of foreign trade. Despite the title, many never developed beyond very small towns, and because of a shift in the run of the economic tide some became sadly decayed monuments to a former prosperity. In the late seventeenth century that change was also bringing into existence a new breed of villages, Burghs of Barony, or it revitalised old ones such as Mauchline. This growth was the first perceptible quickening of the economic pulse in the countryside that would end in the Agricultural Revolution. The Ayrshire that Burns knew had both ancient Burghs such as Ayr, Irvine and Kilmarnock, small Burghs such as Mauchline, and villages such as Tarbolton. All these places would have mixed fortunes during the latter part of the eighteenth century, but they were a vital feature of the landscape.

Burghs had various functions. They concentrated what full-time trades there were. In the Mauchline that Burns knew, among a population of about a thousand there were weavers, joiners, sawyers, masons (including Jean Armour's father), smiths, nail-makers, tanners, and, not least, the trades connected with drink, such as coopers and maltsters. These trades would be fiercely guarded by the local laws so that it would be very difficult for outsiders to muscle in on their livelihoods. The Burgh provided an organised market-place for their products. In these small communities shops did not exist: on the appointed day people would come to the market to seek what they wanted and from those outsiders who had something to sell, the Burgh would levy a *custom* or tax. The unofficial tax on any market day was the dram chased with a *jar* or more of ale that would seal a bargain. In Mauchline alone there were something like thirteen places licensed to sell drink, and enterprising women would – often illegally – brew up ale for market and fair days when the population would be swollen from the surrounding countryside. The opening lines of 'Tam o' Shanter' have raised this into a classic:

> *When chapmen billies leave the street,*
> *And drouthy neebors, neebors meet;*
> *As market-days are wearing late,*
> *An folk begin to tak the gate;*
> *While we sit bousing at the nappy,*
> *An getting fou and unco happy*

Yet the small country Burghs were also centres for a quite different social activity. Tarbolton was the meeting-place of the Bachelors' Club, a debating society founded in 1780 by Robert and Gilbert Burns and at least five others. The most important qualification was 'a frank, honest, open heart; above anything dirty or mean; and must be a professed lover of one or more of the female sex'. Needless to say, Burns was probably the author of that declaration. Tarbolton was also the meeting-place of the St David's Lodge No. 174, where Burns was initiated as a mason in 1781. Mauchline was the meeting-place of a Conversation Society, a debating club that Gilbert Burns attended. There also the local minister lived ('Daddy' or the Rev. William Auld in Burns's time), and there the odd professional person, such as Gavin Hamilton, Burns's lawyer friend, might have an office.

The old-style farming was not something that had been wearing out of fashion: it was breaking down. Various things were combining to make this so, and at the root lay the creep of population growth. More mouths to feed meant a steady growth of ploughed land at the expense of the pasture, and a bigger stock of animals had to be sustained for ploughing. The most vulnerable aspect of the old system was the difficulty of sustaining the livestock through the winter. The range of fodder available was not great. A small amount of hay was made where possible, but it was mostly bog hay, of low nutritional value. Weeds such as thistles were carefully gathered for horse fodder, and any *pease strae* kept for dairy cattle. Straw was required for other uses as well as fodder: thatch, ropes, harness, domestic containers and so on. Once the crop was off the in-by land, the stock could be grazed there, among the stubble, or on patches of growth that had been *haen't* or protected for that purpose. But it was still not enough. Furthermore, the growing cattle trade prompted a swing away from the hardy native sheep, which could sustain themselves better on the short rations available. In all, it pushed the system towards overstocked pasture and arable exhausted by overcropping. Other vital resources such as timber and peat were being depleted far beyond the rate of natural regeneration. The answer lay in two options: a total reorganisation of land use, and alternatives to replace the reliance on local fuel and timber and self-regenerating pasture. The decade in which Robert Burns was born saw this change take root in Ayrshire. What went under the euphemism of *improvement* would be a total revolution of the rural economy, and the Burns family would be firmly caught in that change.

The change in land use broke down the separation of pasture and cultivation, and integrated them in new rotations. The most revolutionary step was to make grass a cultivated crop. The field would be ploughed, harrowed and sown as for any grain crop, but the seed would be grass. The grass would first be harvested as hay, and in later seasons the livestock grazed on it direct, until the time came to plough up the *lye* or lea again. Then it would be sown with a grain crop, and, following that, one of the other innovations would be tried – potatoes or turnips – and the cycle would come round to the sowing of the grass again. The old *muir* would be progressively broken up and brought into cultivation until only the more remote and poor-quality hill ground escaped this spreading tide. This regime was devised by Fairlie, William Burnes's old employer, and it meant that no more than a third of the land and often as little as a quarter would be under crop at any one time. The intensity of cultivation in this new system was thus much less, but it took in much more ground, indeed so much so that what were once little islands of ploughed ground in a sea of *muir* expanded until they joined. Up went the hedges and dykes to separate the livestock on the grass *parks* or enclosed fields from the crops. This was the creation of the countryside we recognise today. In Burns's youth it was entirely and startlingly new.

After seven years at Alloway, the Burnes family left for the farm of Mount Oliphant. Here was the fulfilment of William's ambition to rejoin the ranks of the tenant farmers and regain the position of his forebears. Perhaps because Mount Oliphant was now a nominally improved farm, both William and the laird, Provost Ferguson (of Ayr), expected more than the ground could possibly yield. Looking back, Gilbert remarked with some bitterness that it was 'almost the very poorest soil I know of in a state of cultivation'. So poor was it that in thirty years, during which rental rose considerably elsewhere, at Mount Oliphant it actually dropped. The twelve years the Burns family spent there were a desperate grind, constantly teeter

ing on the edge of disaster. When the ownership of the farm changed hands, the factor for the new owners took a tougher line on the rent than the kindly Provost Ferguson. Burns never forgot that. As Caesar described in 'The Twa Dogs':

> *I've notic'd, on our laird's court-day,*
> *(An monie a time my heart's been wae),*
> *Poor tenant bodies, scant o cash,*
> *How they maun thole a factor's snash:*
> *He'll stamp an threaten, curse an swear*
> *He'll apprehend them, poind their gear;*
> *While they maun staun, wi aspect humble,*
> *An hear it a', an fear an tremble!*

Ellisland is the least changed of all the farms Burns worked. The nearest buildings are, from left to right, byre, barn and house. Nearer is the recently replanted orchard with its restored dyke. Burns built stone dykes here with the abundant but rounded and difficult to use field-stone.

PHOTO: GAVIN SPROTT

The more self-contained nature of the new-style farming regime also bore a penalty, for few people came about the place in the context of work, and it obviously figured in Gilbert's memory as a lonely place. This was compounded in that money was so tight that they could not afford to hire the manpower needed to run the farm. William aged prematurely with the strain, and young Robert did permanent damage to his health in doing

43

The Kitchen at
Mossgiel by Sir
William Allan. The
door on the left leads
to a lobby with access
to the loft, where
Burns slept and did
much of his writing.
Beyond is the *spence*
or best room.
Through the door on
the right is the milk-
house, which gave on
to the byre.

NATIONAL GALLERY OF
SCOTLAND

work too heavy for his growing body.
Everything was pinched, including the
diet, for at Mount Oliphant the Burns
family did not see fresh meat from one
year's end to the next.

Later came Lochlie, Mossgiel, and,
for Robert, Ellisland. However unsatisfac-
tory these other places were, none would
be as bad as Mount Oliphant. Yet they all
had one thing in common. Burns's working life as a farmer was a slog of effecting
change from the old to the new, but getting little of the reward. He understood this well enough himself. As he told his Kincardinshire cousin James
in his letter of 21 June 1783 from Lochlie, 'our landholders, full of ideas of
farming gathered from the English and the Lothian and other soil in Scotland, make no allowance for the odds of the quality of land, and conse-
quently stretch us much beyond in the event, we will be found able to pay'.

The estate was a kingdom within a kingdom. Although subject to the law
of the land, these laws were themselves made collectively by the owners of
the estates. Most of the Scottish countryside was divided so as to be part of
an estate. The number of *bonnet lairds* or working farmers who owned their
land was small. Most of the land was owned by noblemen, gentlemen of
ancient family, or, increasingly in Burns's day, men whose wealth had ena-
bled them to rise into land ownership and gentility. In Ayrshire there were
several large estates such as those of the Earls of Loudon and Eglinton. The
estate of Auchinleck, where James Boswell came from, was of large to medium size, comprising over twenty thousand acres. Although a portion of
this estate was intractable hill land, after improvement it had over one hundred farms. Within his estate, the laird and his lady were as sovereign and
consort, and the factor their appointed prime minister. The land was theirs,
and if there was to be any serious change to the way it was used, that change
had to start with the laird.

The capital required was considerable, because the switch-over was a
labour of Hercules, involving as it did the clearing of stones and weeds, the
realignment of the *rigs* or cultivation ridges into neat fifteen-feet-wide strips
in tidy squared-off fields, the putting in of drains, and the hand-trenching
of old pasture, to mention but a few of the tasks. The prime objective was
to improve the state of the soil sufficiently for the new sown grass to flourish,
which was impossible on the unimproved sour and wet ground, and this

meant extensive liming. To make progress in this endeavour depended on the creation of a virtually new transport system, for not only had the lime to be brought to the countryside, but also, in the earlier days, before centralised limekilns were built, the coal to burn it. This again depended on action by the landed interest, in the case of Ayrshire securing the Turnpike Acts of 1766 and 1774, and then putting up the capital. These roads, along which the improved two-wheeled *box-cairts* went, also opened up access to markets and the import of badly needed timber, or even the rich midden contents from towns and villages.

However, the renting of land under the new system was very far from the farmer hiring a commodity. The *tack* or lease would impose strict conditions, such as the imposition of the Fairlie rotation. It was also a form of partnership, in which the laird provided the land and the farmer provided the stock. As the scale of the new farms was bigger, so was that of the capital required to stock them. At Mount Oliphant the stocking required over twice the sum of the annual rental. Some of that stock must have gone into Lochlie, supplemented by an advance from the laird, but much of what William made from that venture was consumed in his legal battle with the same man. What remained of the family's savings went into stocking Mossgiel. However, two poor seasons, bad seed and animal disease severely depleted that money also; and so when Gilbert remained as sole tenant he only survived because Robert diverted a sizeable portion of the money he had made out of the Edinburgh edition of his poems to re-stock it. The laird still had his capital and got his rent. If this was the brave new world of *improvement*, it must have seemed no fairer than the old one. As Burns said in his 'Epistle' to Davie Sillar:

> It's hardly in a body's pow'r,
> To keep, at times, frae being sour,
> To see how things are shar'd

Robert's was the third generation to find itself in a financial pickle. In the end, he left the land, and also left his family in relative prosperity, yet the spectre of ruin was always there, even in the delirium of his final illness. The conformist Gilbert accepted this as normal, and went on to become a faithful servant of the system as a factor. Robert did not. Besides being a farmer and then exciseman, he created for himself a unique alternative: as he styled it, the office of 'his bardship'.

CHAPTER THREE

ON FAITH, MORALS
AND MARRIAGE

❧❧❧❧❧❧❧❧❧❧❧❧❧❧❧❧❧❧❧❧❧❧❧❧❧❧❧❧❧❧

The number of genuinely irreligious people in eighteenth-century Scotland must have been very small, and Robert Burns was not among them. In his work he makes numerous references to some form of deity, and sometimes ventures an agnostic suspicion of 'old-wife prejudices and tales!'. As he put it in a letter to Robert Muir on 7 March 1789, 'every age and every nation has a different set of stories: and the many are always weak, of consequence they have often, perhaps always been deceived'. Whatever Burns's attitude to religion, it was not bred of casual ignorance. His father's *Manual of Religious Belief in the form of a dialogue between Father and Son* is touching evidence that William had laboured to see his son 'drawn by the conviction of a Man, not the halter of an Ass', as Robert later put it to Mrs Dunlop in his letter of 1 January 1789. Yet Burns knew his Bible with a thoroughness that verged on the encyclopedic. This was not just the reach of a remarkable memory or familiarity bred of pious study. It caught his imagination. As he said to Bishop Skinner, the son of 'Tullochgorm', the Rev. John Skinner, he had early become familiar with 'the old bards of the best of all poetical books – the Old Testament'. There is little in the human experience that is not spelt out in that huge store of narrative.

As we will see later, the Reformation in Scotland was driven initially by a dislike of a top-heavy establishment where the higher clergy were remote and the parish ministry poverty-stricken and ineffective. The reformers got the result they had intended. Whatever the form of church government, whether under the government-sponsored *prelates* or bishops of the Episcopal system, or the rabid theocrats of Covenanting Presbyterianism, the parish minister was faced not just with a congregation, but a jury.

The spirit of Presbyterian theocracy was maintained by the Scottish revolution settlement of 1689, because the Episcopalians gave Dutch William cause to think that a Presbyterian settlement would serve him better. That pushed Episcopalians into the Jacobite camp, and identified the Presbyterians with the new deal of what eventually became known as the 'Glorious Revolution', when in 1688 James VII was chased off his throne. But following the Union of the Scottish and English Parliaments in 1707, the now English-dominated legislature proceeded to interfere. In 1712 the Toleration Act made life easier for the Episcopal party that had lost out in 1689, but also opened the road to every expression of schismatic fancy. At the same time, the Patronage Act severely restricted a congregation's power of choice over its minister by handing much of that power back to the *heritors*: in effect, the landowners. Over the years this would alter the basic character of the established Kirk; ministers increasingly reflected the values of worldly as well as spiritual authority. As the eighteenth century wore on, a theologically aware population voted with its feet. Those who felt strongly enough set up new congregations and new denominations outside the establishment, and that included an extraordinary range. On the one hand were the fire-breathing Cameronians, who represented the ultimate vision of a nation in a marriage contract with God, and who saw themselves as the suffering and bleeding remnant of the true Kirk of Scotland. In 1740 an evangelical party within the establishment who could no longer put up with the system of appointing ministers was pushed out of the main body, and became the first 'seceders', rapidly building up an alternative organisation, but one which only four years later would split further and recede into the mind set of the previous century. A quite different and liberal group started in 1761, Thomas Gillespie's Relief Presbytery, for those 'oppressed in their Christian privileges' by narrow legalistic dogma.

A later age would look back on all this schism in puzzlement, but for Burns and his generation it was familiar. Armed and armoured with erudition, the different groups strove not just with the Devil, but with one another, and their departure from the established Kirk left the Moderates in charge, and by Burns's time they had come to dominate. On one level morally correct, on another urbane and easy-going, the Moderates reflected the attitudes of the Enlightenment. That was one reason why the break-away groups despised them, but, if anything, Burns took their part, not in a partisan spirit, but because at best they reflected a sane breath of toleration and broader interests. One such, John McMath, requested a copy of 'Holy Willie's Prayer', which was already going from hand to hand in Ayrshire. Burns sent not just a copy, but a letter in verse:

47

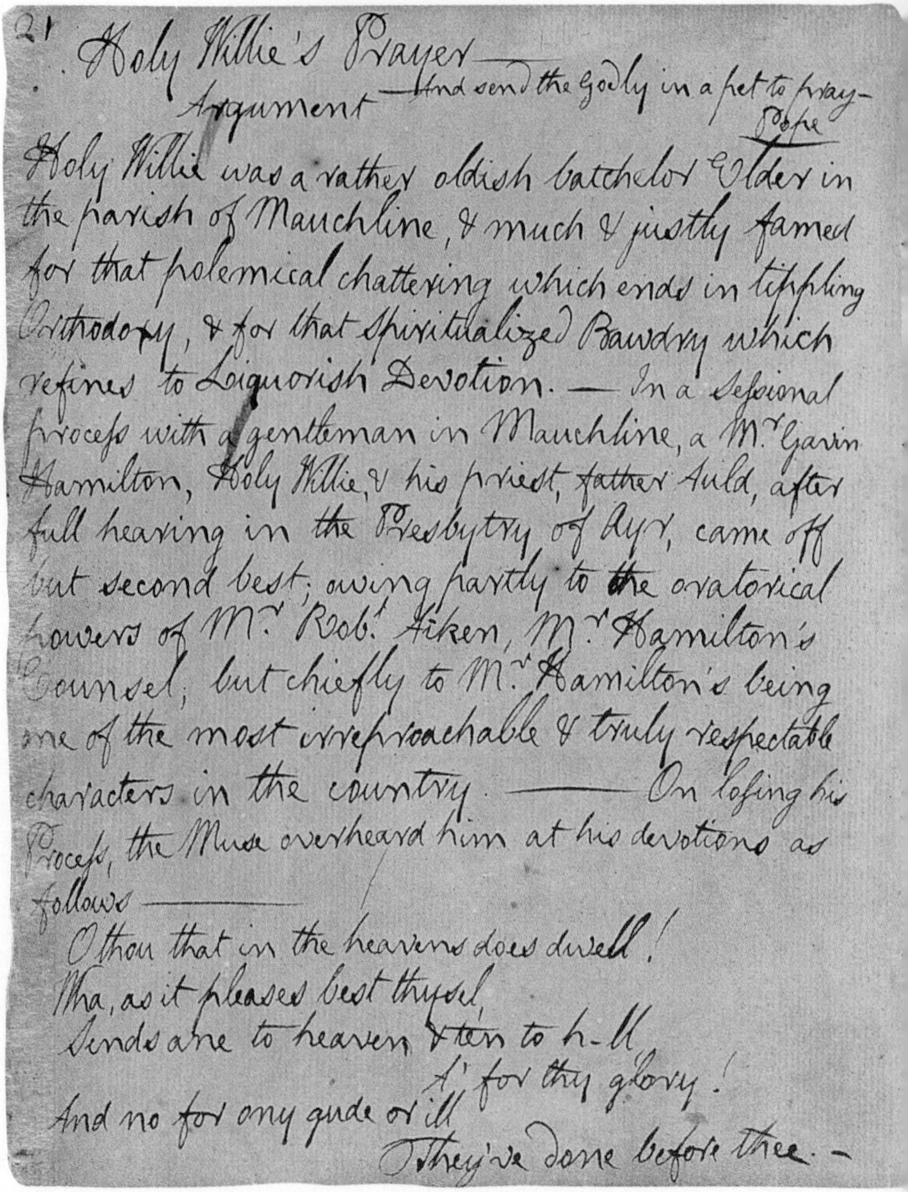

21 Holy Willie's Prayer —

Argument — And send the godly in a pet to pray — Pope

Holy Willie was a rather oldish batchelor Elder in the parish of Mauchline, & much & justly famed for that polemical chattering which ends in tippling Orthodoxy, & for that Spiritualized Bawdry which refines to Liquorish Devotion. — In a Sessional process with a gentleman in Mauchline, a Mr Gavin Hamilton, Holy Willie, & his priest, father Auld, after full hearing in the Presbytry of Ayr, came off but second best; owing partly to the oratorical powers of Mr Robt Aiken, Mr Hamilton's Counsel; but chiefly to Mr Hamilton's being one of the most irreproachable & truly respectable characters in the country. —— On losing his Process, the Muse overheard him at his devotions as follows ——

O thou that in the heavens does dwell!
Wha, as it pleases best thysel,
Sends ane to heaven & ten to h-ll,
A' for thy glory!
And no for ony gude or ill
They've done before thee. —

Two pages of 'Holy Willie's Prayer' in Burns's own hand. Manuscript copies of his poems circulated widely in south-west Scotland, before a selection of them entitled *Poems Chiefly in the Scottish Dialect* was printed at Kilmarnock on 31 July 1786. However, 'Holy Willie's Prayer' was not included: it was still considered too controversial.

NATIONAL LIBRARY OF SCOTLAND: MS. 86.

22

I bless & praise thy matchless might,
When thousands thou has left in night,
That I am here before thy sight,
   For gifts & grace,
A burning & a shining light
   To a' this place. —

What was I, or my generation,
That I should get such exaltation?
I, wha deserv'd most just damnation,
   For broken laws
Sax thousand years ere my creation
   Thro' Adam's cause?

When from my mother's womb I fell,
Thou might hae plunged me deep in hell,
To gnash my gooms, & weep, & wail,
   In burning lakes,
Where damned devils roar & yell
   Chain'd to their stakes. —

Yet I am here, a chosen sample,
To shew thy grace is great & ample:
I'm here, a pillar o' thy temple
   Strong as a rock,
A guide, a ruler & example
   To a' thy flock. —

But I gae mad at their grimaces,
Their sighin, cantin, grace-proud faces,
Their three-mile prayers, an hauf-mile graces,
Their raxin conscience,
Whase greed, revenge, an pride disgraces
Waur nor their nonsense.

TO THE REV. JOHN MCMATH

Other religionists who had been maligned by the die-hards got Burns's support:

Sour Bigotry on his last legs
Girns an looks back,
Wishing the ten Egyptian plagues
May seize you quick.

EPISTLE TO JOHN GOLDIE

However, it was not bigotry that was on its last legs, but what had become of the orthodox interpretation of Calvinist doctrine, and the God who on some mysterious personal whim:

Sends ane to Heaven, an ten to Hell,
A' for Thy glory,
And no for onie guid or ill
They've done before Thee!

HOLY WILLIE'S PRAYER

Although Burns made sport of Calvinist orthodoxy, his enemy was far from beaten. A mental habit of generations would live on long after him, and to this day is far from dead. People can still find in Burns's satire a personal liberation – from something that they have inherited from past generations but still carry within them.

John Mair was born in 1469 in Gleghornie near North Berwick in East Lothian. He went to Haddington Grammar School, and then travelled widely, studying at the universities of Glasgow, Oxford, Cambridge and then Paris. John Mair, or Major, as he became known, was one of the foremost intellects of the day. Besides his *History of Greater Britain* in 1521, he wrote a commentary on the Four Gospels published in 1529, defending the Roman Church against the theories of John Wycliffe, Jan Hus and

Martin Luther. Major would remain faithful to the old Kirk until his death at St Andrews in 1550. He wanted to reform it from within, yet had what were radical views for the time, maintaining that the people were the true source of civil power.

One of John Major's pupils at the Collège de Montaigu in Paris in the late 1520s was a young Jean Calvin from Noyon in Picardy. By that time Europe was in the uproar started by Martin Luther in 1517 when he nailed his criticisms of the Pope to a church door in Wittenberg in Germany. Because he tried to understand those whom he opposed, Major was one of Calvin's main sources for the theoretical framework of the reformers' thinking. What had enraged Luther was the sale of 'indulgences'. In crude terms 'indulgences' provided a remission of sins for a cash payment; it was no more than a money-making racket. In intellectual terms Luther was tilting at a windmill. But what he rediscovered was the 'doctrine of grace', the central plank of the Reformation. Man should not presume to shove and push God to look favourably on humankind by a parade of good behaviour, much less cash payments. What Adam had messed up God had restored in Christ. All people had to do was respond to that unique act of divine generosity and their spirit would be reborn, their hearts would change and the rest would find its place. An act of free will as we might understand it had nothing to do with it, because unredeemed people in the thrall of sin do not have that kind of control over themselves, they can only pleiter on through the mire of sin. But God is seeking His people out, the initiative is His. The early reformers did not concern themselves overly with notions of 'predestination'; that is, that some are fated to be touched by grace and others left out. If anything it was a counsel of comfort and assurance that the Divinity was striding out over the hill in confident certainty, as the shepherd who knew exactly where he would find lost sheep.

Settling in Geneva in Switzerland, Calvin became the arch theoretician of the reformers, setting out his thoughts in his *Institutes of the Christian Religion*, which he first published in 1539, with the final version in 1559. It was a monumental work, in the same league as Augustine's *Confessions* and Marx's *Das Kapital*. One of Calvin's pupils – and also one of Major's when he was professor of philosophy and theology at Glasgow – was John Knox, and he brought the teachings of his master to Scotland. But they did not survive in their original form. Calvin's successor, Theodore Beza, and the following generation of divines, including those in Scotland such as Andrew Melville and Robert Rollock, 'developed' Calvin's theology so that one fundamental changed. For Calvin and Knox, repentance was something that flowed from forgiveness, the proper human reaction to the outstretched

hand, not the condition that went before it. But now this was stood on its
head. If you repent, then God will forgive you. What a terrible abyss now
opened before the supplicant for salvation! How much repentance was
necessary? God would know, but the hapless penitent could never know. In
an ironic paradox, it was back to the days of 'indulgences', with cash
payments changed for an infinitely harsher tribute, the fencing in of the
running fires of doubt with legalistic trenches of 'correct' behaviour. At
worst, morality lost that spontaneous sense of a nobility of the spirit for its
own sake, and became a mere firebreak against the wrath of God, and Life
was reduced to Standard Living Procedure. In Scotland this reached a high
tide of theocratic puritanism between 1648 and 1651, the so-called 'Second
Reformation'. The harsh discipline of the revolutionaries was destructive.
The wholesale importation of English Puritan usages, which shouldered
aside the spirit and character of Knox's Reformation more surely than any
high-church meddling by an anglicised Charles I, left a tough new orthodoxy
that would persist, because it was also entwined with an emergent political
philosophy. Burns rejected the theology, and, as we shall see, was an ardent
disciple of the political philosophy that grew out of it.

The deficiency of a theology that had become a product of fear and
legalism was that it differed little from a morality bred of common sense
and mutual convenience. Such a morality is founded on the simple and
practical question: what if? What if no one tells the truth? What if no one
keeps agreements? This is not the product of faith, but of rationality. It is in
the realm of what was then called 'natural law'. Any religion that pitches its
camp in the same territory will have to fight it out with reason on equal
terms. In the eighteenth century the spread of the Enlightenment meant
intellectual bruisers such as David Hume in the field. The man at the tail of
the plough would hardly halt at the endrig to thumb his way through *An
Enquiry Concerning Human Understanding*, but he would hear the artillery
slugging it out. This was usually a one-sided cannonade on the part of the
defenders, some of their guns trained on the infidels of reason, and the
others – most of them – pointed at their own troops to keep them in order.
It was as if the fabric of the belief was imploding, leaving the defending
ministers to a bitter and even dishonest scrap over the surface details:

> *Ev'n ministers, they hae been kend,*
> *In holy rapture,*
> *A rousing whid at times to vend,*
> *And nail't wi Scripture.*

DEATH AND DOCTOR HORNBOOK

Burns did not have some grand counter-structure to put in its place, but he had his personal alternative. As he confessed to Mrs Dunlop in his letter of 1 January 1789, he longed for a certain freedom and expression of the spirit that was to be found elsewhere:

The first Sunday of May; a breezy blue-skyed noon some time about the beginning, & a hoary morning & calm sunny day about the end, of Autumn; these, time out of mind, have been with me a kind of Holidays. – Not like the Sacramental, Executioner-face of a Kilmarnock Communion; but to laugh or cry, be chearful or pensive, moral, or devout, according to the mood & tense of the Season & myself.

One such season in Burns's poetic imagination was 'The Cotter's Saturday Night'. Here is no grinding theological apparatus, no *Treatise on Effectual Calling* (Robert Rollock, 1596), with its Covenants of Works and Covenants of Grace. The meal is a cheerful but wholesome affair, shadowing the Christian fellowship in the body of Christ expressed in the sacrament of communion. Then they turn to The Word, embodying as it does the law and the prophets. But the sequence is quite clear. In this, Burns was truer to the spirit of the original Reformation than the cohorts of orthodoxy, drawing on a quiet but broad subterranean stream that still informed the personal attitudes of the many hopeful spiritual travellers who next to the Bible kept John Bunyan's *Pilgrim's Progress*.

Burns reconstructed what might be called a kind of personal, secular 'theology' which liberated his mental energy just as the rediscovery of 'grace' had liberated the early reformers. He had his own peculiar version of The Fall: 'We come onto this world with a heart and disposition to do good for it' until dragged down by prudence 'to the blackguard Sterling of ordinary currency' (Letter to Mrs Dunlop, 2 August 1788). The antidote lay in the cult of 'sensibility'.

The high priest of this movement was Henry Mackenzie, and the attitude was expressed in his novel *The Man of Feeling*, published in 1771. Hardly readable now, the book would have been long forgotten but for Burns's interest in the underlying idea. In Mackenzie's novel that idea was the exercise of pity and generosity towards the victims of a cruel world, a work-out of emotional piety. With Burns, sensibility grew to stand for the honest response and feeling of the whole person, a kind of super-awareness of the heart. This was Burns's personal 'doctrine of grace'; it suffused all of his writings, and affected his personal morality. His satire did much more than burn the dreich temples of orthodox Calvinism, it cleared the ground

Francis Grose
(1731–91) by John
Kay.
A retired army
captain, Grose had
written the
*Antiquities of
England and Wales*
(1773–87). When he
visited Ayrshire to
research *The
Antiquities of Scotland*
he met Burns and
they became fast
friends. He is credited
with inspiring Burns
to write 'Tam o'
Shanter', which was
first published in the
Edinburgh Magazine
in March 1791.
Reproduced from *A
Series of Original
Portraits* by John Kay
(Edinburgh, 1877).

for the attitude he expressed. When people complain that Burns can become a religion, they are sometimes nearer the mark than they think.

From the 1930s a belief grew in literary circles that the Reformation had destroyed something essential in the spirit of Scotland that had never been recovered. In his 'Scotland 1941' Edwin Muir expressed this in words that sob with rage:

> *A simple sky roofed in that rustic day,*
> *The busy corn-fields and the haunted holms,*
> *The green road winding up the ferny brae.*
> *But Knox and Melville clapped their preaching palms*
> *And bundled all the harvesters away,*
> *Hoodicrow Peden in the blighted corn*
> *Hacked with his rusty beak the starving haulms.*
> *Out of that desolation we were born.*

The charge was that the reformed Kirk was a jealous and joyless monster that had savaged the natural music of the soul. In abolishing the old festivals of Yule and *Pace* or Easter it had destroyed the foci of song and merriment for the people, and thus much of the folk culture. The names of Whitsunday and Martinmas very much survived, but only to mark the periods of work. Then people would leave one tenancy or service and start another. In the same way, Candlemas was a time for yoking the plough, Lammas-tide for winning the hay.

There is some truth in this, for the abolition of these festivals as part of religion was a fact. But behind the old Kirk festivals lay another enemy: superstition. The target was not enjoyment in itself, but a serious pagan rival. The old Christian festivals were to the reformers a front for the iniquities of the Golden Calf. Behind the *Invention* (ie Discovery) of the Cross was *Beltane,* then believed to refer to Baal's Fire. Yule, the old name for Christmas, was pagan anyway. The *Johnsmas* fires of midsummer and the *bleize* on Halloween were equally abominable.

The divide in belief was real. In the old country communities, just as problems had to be coped with locally, so did the explanations have to be provided. People were as impatient of uncertainty then as they are now. There had to be a reason for things. When disaster struck, such as animal disease, the explanation did not stop at 'an act of God'. For the reformers, the logical response was that the community had caused offence to the Almighty, and a public day of 'humiliation and prayer' would be announced

*While we sit bousing
at the nappy,
An' gettin fou and
unco happy.*

A scene from *Tam o'
Shanter and Souter
Johnny . . .
illustrated by Thomas
Landseer* (London,
1830).
In the nineteenth
century Burns's
poems and songs
went through many
editions in the press,
and Academicians
vied with jobbing
artists to gratify the
public's taste for
illustrations to
accompany them.
'Tam o' Shanter' fired
many an artistic
imagination.

NATIONAL LIBRARY OF
SCOTLAND

in which douce country folk were urged to forsake the fleshpots of Egypt
for the moral hygiene of the desert.

For those still cleaving to the old superstitions, the reaction was entirely different. The same procedure would be followed as in the creation of
the Beltane fire of spring. All the fires in the district would be put out and
fresh fire – *needfire* as it was called (the derivation is uncertain) – would be
kindled by rubbing two sticks together. Once a roaring bonfire had been
built up, it would be divided to create a passage through it, and the cattle
would be driven between the flames to *sain* or cleanse them. In the Highlands, where the established Kirk was much weaker, such remedies were
tried well into the eighteenth century. Remarkably, in Ayrshire itself, that
heartland of Covenanting piety, a Johnsmas fire blazed every year on the
Moat Hill at Tarbolton until 1927.

The Kirk's implacable dislike of these activities was not only against
the superstition itself, but also that they were communal acts. Turning to
the fires of Baal rather than mass repentance might provoke such bolts of
divine displeasure as hardly bore thinking about, such as the plagues the
Lord had visited on the recalcitrant Egyptians. It was playing out the theme
of conditional grace on a grand scale. Dreadful famines attended the closing years of the seventeenth century, yet some ministers were alarmed at
the resilience with which the population recovered its spirit. It was feared

The doubling storm roars thro the woods;
The lightnings flash from pole to pole.

Engraving by William Forrest, after an original drawing by Samuel Bough. From *The Works of Robert Burns*, edited by William Scott Douglas (Edinburgh, 1877–9).

NATIONAL LIBRARY OF SCOTLAND

that such rash levity could start the whole grim process over again.

Years of shortage there would be, with months of perishing hunger and malnutrition. In the early part of 1796 there were riots in the streets of Dumfries over the severe shortage of meal, but in the Lowlands there was never again overt famine. The growth of trade, the painful but steady advance into improved agriculture, the broader horizons and opportunities of a bigger world demolished the old, closed-in superstitions.

This may have been happening in Burns's day, but the process was far from complete. The Kirk could put a stop to public acts that it deemed relics of the old papistical superstitions and pagan rites, but it was harder to break into the private personal world where belief was passed on within families. Betty Davidson was a cousin of Agnes Brown, Robert's mother, and she came to stay with the family from time to time at Alloway to help Agnes with her cheese-making business. She had an extraordinary store of strange tales and beliefs with which she frightened and entertained the children. As Burns wrote to Dr John Moore in his autobiographical letter of 2 August 1787, this had

> *so strong an effect on my imagination, that to this hour, in my nocturnal rambles, I sometimes keep a sharp look-out in suspicious places; and though nobody can be more sceptical in these matters than I, yet it often takes an effort of Philosophy to shake off these idle terrors.*

Although Burns would always have his feet planted in the rational world, he never lost his insight into that archaic half-lit region of *freats* and *notions*. He recorded them as something passing, yet conveyed the sense of a different mind-set. The whisky-soaked vision of the *guidman* of Shanter is the most famous example, but 'Halloween', although more detached, is also a more systematic description, the explanatory notes that Burns wrote as fascinating as the poem is fun. Here superstition has stuck to that inner world that defies rational prediction, and in particular the relationship between the sexes. Long after the poem was written, young people would still *haud Halloween* and in the spring roll their bannocks to see with whom they would be partnered for life. In William Burnes's north east, a hint of old horrors would remain on the lips of children as they went round seeking fuel for the Halloween *bleize* shouting 'Gie's a peat tae burn the witches!'.

And, vow! Tam saw an unco sight!
Warlocks and witches in a dance.

Engraving after a painting by John Faed.
From *Tam o' Shanter* (1855).
NATIONAL LIBRARY OF SCOTLAND

Although we might not expect it, this world of the supernatural is very physical. It is connected with events and quite specific places:

> And near the thorn, aboon the well,
> Whare Mungo's mither hang'd hersel.
>
> TAM O' SHANTER

In the ballad 'Tam Lin', which Burns collected for the *Scots Musical Museum*, the elements are all intensely physical – water, fire, plants, and the very place itself:

> O I forbid you, maidens a'
> That wear gowd on your hair,
> To come, or gae by Carterhaugh,
> For young Tom-lin is there.

'Tam Lin' is one of the most extraordinary ballads that Burns collected. The frontiers of time and place and the natural world part to reveal familiar things in a different light. It is the tale of the love between Tam Lin and Janet, and how she retrieves Tam from the Abyss.

> The queen o Fairies she caught me,
> In yon green hill to dwell,
> And pleasant is the fairy-land;
> But, an eerie tale to tell!
>
> Ay at the end of seven years
> We pay a tiend to hell;
> I am sae fair and fu of flesh
> I'm fear'd it be mysel.
> . . . . .
> But the night is Halloween, lady,
> The morn is Hallowday;
> Then win me, win me, an ye will,
> For weel I wat ye may.

The carlin claught her by the rump,
And left poor Maggie scarce a stump.

Anonymous engraving from *The Illustrated Family Burns* (New York, 1879).

The story turns on a symbolically described but barely concealed physical union between Janet and Tam that is startling in its directness:

> They'll turn me to a bear sae grim,
> And then a lion bold;

But hold me fast and fear me not,
As ye shall love your child.

Again they'll turn me in your arms
To a red het gaud of airn;
But hold me fast and fear me not,
I'll do you nae harm.

And last they'll turn me, in your arms,
Into the burning lead;
Then throw me into well-water,
O throw me in wi speed!

Tam is pleading with the maiden Janet to trust him and the potentially frightening side of a man's sexual expression. There is no boundary between love, sex and the begetting of children. Burns was exposed to this attitude by his mother. As she sang to her children:

O, kissin is the key o love
An clappin is the lock;
An makin of's the best thing,
That e'er a young thing got.

O, CAN YE LABOUR LEA –

The sure way to Burns's heart was through song. Helen Blair, the first girl he admired, sang sweetly, enough to prod him to fit his own words to the music. His Jean also had a fine singing voice, and it was Jessie Lewars singing 'The Robin cam' to the Wren's nest' as she helped nurse Burns in his last illness that inspired his last Scots song, 'O, Wert thou in the Cauld Blast'. It is not just a love song, but contains a tender paternal element, the keepsake of a dying man for the brightness and energy of youth.

In the eighteenth-century countryside the energy of youth was simply directed. For young people there was work – and the *courtin*. If people imagine that the late twentieth century has some monopoly in a consuming interest in sex, they are mistaken. In Burns's day, all the rituals connected with courtship, rituals predicting who would marry and when, the opportunities opened up by dancing, the songs, the giving of love tokens, the making of trysts, not to mention the physical get-together, all this was the principal enjoyment open to young people, and for many probably the only one.

What was changing in Burns's day were not the values, but the social controls by which they were enforced. On the one hand was the tight family circle of 'The Cotter's Saturday Night', where one of the daughters brings home her lad for the first time:

> *Wi kindly welcome, Jenny brings him ben;*
> *A strappin youth, he takes the mother's eye;*
> *Blythe Jenny sees the visit's no ill-taen;*
> *The father cracks of horses, pleughs, and kye.*
> *The youngster's artless heart o'erflows wi joy,*
> *But blate and laithfu, scarce can weel behave;*
> *The mother, wi a woman's wiles, can spy*
> *What makes the youth sae bashfu and sae grave;*
> *Weel-pleas'd to think her bairn's respected like the lave.*

That was how the Burnes family were brought up. With the possible exception of his brief stay at Kirkoswald, where a prosperous trade in contraband made it a wild place and where the teenage lad beheld novel scenes of 'roaring dissipation', Burns was restrained in sexual matters until his twenty-third year. It is not just that Burns was 'an affa man wi the lassies', as the phrase still puts it. New opportunities presented themselves when he won free of his father's control.

Burns's experience was true in a more general way, and stemmed from economic change. The virtuous young lad in 'The Cotter's Saturday Night' might have been from a neighbouring cotter's family and still subject to family discipline. Within Burns's lifetime he would have become a farm servant, like one of those in 'The Inventory', lodging with his employer and perhaps sleeping above the stable or another part of the steadings:

> *For men, I've three mischievous boys,*
> *Run-deils for fechtin an for noise …*
> *… I rule them, as I ought, discreetly,*
> *An aften labour them completely;*
> *An ay on Sundays duly, nightly,*
> *I on the* Questions *tairge them tightly …*

Not all masters would take such trouble. And as Burns adds:

> *I've nane in female servan' station,*
> *(Lord keep me ay frae a' temptation!)*

As the labour structure changed in the countryside, so did the farm servant housing. In the Lowlands between the Forth and the Moray Firth a whole system was taking root about or just after Burns's time, where in many areas single men were housed in barrack-like bothies that were part of the steadings. The bothy men had a strong group identity and a fearsome work ethic, but also cultivated a devil-may-care independence that scoffed at moral interference. Pregnancy out of wedlock was commonplace among country girls.

Not that pre-marital pregnancy was rare before this time. The law of Scotland virtually licensed pre-marital sex, because subsequent marriage legitimised any offspring, a survival from the old pre-Reformation canon law. Marriage was not something imposed by an act of officialdom, it was a personal covenant between the woman and the man. After this fashion Burns first 'married' Jean Armour. The weakness of this arrangement in law lay in the want of witnesses, either in a spoken covenant or a witnessed document.

Thus the road was open for couples to enjoy their physical union first and complete the formalities if and when the woman became pregnant. The number of children conceived out of wedlock but born within it was

The Holy Fair, Mauchline, by Alexander Carse. Holy Fairs were outdoor preachings held in preparation for the communion service, and might take place twice a year. They attracted all sorts, including youths whose devotional interest was with the opposite sex.

enormous. Even then, this trend was not straightforward. Privacy was something of a luxury. A common theme in Burns's songs is the resort to quiet places in the countryside for the *tryst* or meeting.

Control was also slipping over the initial places of meeting. The harvest field and the *kirn* that might follow (the kind of celebration which is the setting of 'Mary Morrison') were increasingly rivalled by the scenes described in 'The Holy Fair'. Here was pointed paradox indeed, for against the backdrop of a religious gathering with relays of book-pounding preachers:

> *Here sits a raw o tittlin jads,*
> *Wi heavin breasts an bare neck;*
> *An there a batch o wabster lads,*
> *Blackguardin frae Kilmarnock,*
> *For fun this day.*

And at the finish:

> *An monie jobs that day begin,*
> *May end in houghmagandie*
> *Some ither day.*

As the trail of natural children showed, Burns was no stranger to the *houghmagandie* himself. Yet when the inevitable happened, as with Betty Paton, there was still no split between physical enjoyment and his affection for woman and child:

> *Sweet fruit o monie a merry dint,*
> *My funny toil is no a' tint,*
> *Tho thou cam to the warl' asklent*
> A POET'S WELCOME TO HIS LOVE-BEGOTTEN DAUGHTER

The modern view of fornication still owes much to the attitude developed in the late eighteenth century among 'respectable' people that the man seduced and ruined the woman. This was not necessarily the view held by the other ranks of society. Eve with her rosy-cheeked apple offered carnal as well as intellectual knowledge. It may have been a male presumption, for we have little or no evidence from the other half of humanity, but the presumption was there. As the soldier's widow sings in 'The Jolly Beggars':

The Black Stool by David Allan. The Kirk Sessions, or church courts, punished sinners by requiring them to occupy a special seat during services as an act of penance – thus exposing them to public censure. When Burns first fell foul of the Mauchline Kirk Session over his relationship with Jean Armour he was spared the 'creepy chair', but made to stand in his pew on three successive Sundays.

NATIONAL GALLERY OF SCOTLAND

I once was a maid, tho I cannot tell when,
And still my delight is in proper young men ...

The *Merry Muses of Caledonia* enlarge on this theme in graphic detail. The situations described are gross, often absurd and can be very funny, and the fun is frequently at the expense of the man who cannot satisfy a woman's natural appetite. Early biographers suppressed Burns's letter to Bob Ainslie of 3 March 1788, describing his reunion with Jean Armour after his return from Edinburgh. After sorting out various other matters, her claims on himself (which he stubbornly denied), her accommodation, even her furniture and her aliment:

I have f—d til she rejoiced with joy unspeakable and full of glory ... Oh, what a peacemaker is a guid weel-willy pintle! It is the mediator, the guarantee, the umpire, the bond of union, the solemn league and covenant ... and Tree of Life between Man and Woman.

Later biographers have passed lofty judgement on the poet for what they deem his scandalous disregard for the welfare of Jean and the imminently expected twins, and have indeed blamed Robert for the infants' deaths. Rash though the encounter was, recent research in 1992 by Dr James Mackay in his *Biography of Robert Burns* (pp. 402–3) has suggested that this incident and the birth of the twins were sufficiently far apart for there to be no connection between it and their subsequent demise. What has escaped attention is Robert's report of Jean's apparent sexual enjoyment, dismissed out of hand as mere *braggadocio* or empty boasting.

The *braggadocio* refers to the man's capacity to do the necessary:

> *'Come rede me, dame, come tell me dame,*
> *My dame come tell me truly,*
> *What length of graith, when weel ca'd hame,*
> *Will sair a woman duly?'*
> *The carlin clew her wanton tail,*
> *Her wanton tail sae ready –*
> *I learn'd a sang in Annandale,*
> *Nine inch will please a lady ...*
>
> COME REDE ME, DAME

But Burns could see beyond this. One popular version of 'John Anderson' which he collected for the *Merry Muses* describes the sour mirth of a woman whose husband is past it:

> *John Anderson, my jo, John,*
> *When first that ye began,*
> *Ye had as good a tail-tree,*
> *As ony ither man;*
> *But now it's waxen wan, John,*
> *And wrinkles to and fro;*
> *I've twa gae-ups for ae gae-down,*
> *John Anderson, my jo.*

He took this rather dismal situation and quite transformed it. In Burns's well-known version of 'John Anderson', after looking back on youthful pleasure the woman concludes:

> *Now we maun totter down, John,*
> *And hand in hand we'll go,*
> *And sleep thegither at the foot,*
> *John Anderson my jo!*

This poem is extraordinary in several ways, for it turns base metal into gold. It is a convincing love-song of an old woman to an old man who had come to the end of their lives together, and yet it was composed by one not even in his middle years. It balances the joys of youth against the pleasures of memory in old age.

It was not unknown for Oxford dons declining into a senile adolescence to quarrel over which of Jane Austen's heroines was the most desirable. A vaguely similar process haunts the ghosts of the various women Robert Burns took up with. The difference is that here we are dealing with real people, who were as they were and not as we would have them. Yet even when we try to form a true picture of what they were like, as in the case of Jean Armour, whom Robert married, it is not easy. Not that she could have been a shadowy figure in her lifetime. Through all the vicissitudes, even when Burns swore that he was not going to marry her formally after all, and even after he expressed outright rejection on his second return from Edinburgh, he kept returning to her, to 'that delicious armful'. John Syme, one of Burns's friends in Dumfries, hinted that it would require poetic imagination to discern Jean's bonniness; however, his view was that of a man whose gentlemanly background perhaps found attraction in cultivated refinement and not elsewhere. 'Bonie Jean' inspired fourteen songs. We can only infer what she might have looked like as a young woman, and before frequent childbirth and hard work had taken its toll on her figure, since the first likenesses of her are in middle age, when she was described as 'still very comely'. It is possible to imagine that in her twenties she was indeed pretty and sexy, rather than beautiful, with her regular features, high cheekbones, luxuriant hair and dark eyes.

Burns's friends such as William Smellie would enquire kindly after 'Jean and the bairnies'. She was described as a person of practical good sense, and her widowhood was marked by a dignity and maturity that impressed the constant stream of curious visitors. Burns's own sober assessment is an interesting one. Writing to Peggy Chalmers on 16 September 1788, he stated that his recent marriage to Jean 'was not in consequence of the attachment of romance perhaps; but I had a long and much-loved fellow creature's happiness or misery in my determination ... Nor have I any cause to repent it ... I have got the handsomest figure, the sweetest temper, the soundest constitution, and the kindest heart in the county'. Burns enjoyed being married. As he put it to his Edinburgh friend, Alexander Cunningham, in a letter of 10 September 1792:

Jean Armour, Mrs Robert Burns (1767–1834), with Sarah, her favourite granddaughter, after a painting by Samuel Mackenzie. This picture shows Jean in middle age. What might 'that delicious armful' have looked like when she first caught Robert's eye? Cropping the engraving (below) gives us some clue.

From *The Land of Burns* by John Wilson and Robert Chambers (Glasgow, 1840).

how do you like, I mean really *like, the Married Life? — Ah, my Friend! Matrimony is quite a different thing from what your love-sick youths & sighing girls take it to be! ... I shall give you* my *ideas of the Conjugal State. ... Well then, the scale of Good-wife ship I divide into ten parts. – Good nature, four; Good-sense, two; Wit, one; Personal Charms, viz. a sweet face, eloquent eyes, fine limbs, graceful carriage, (I would add a fine waist too, but that is so soon spoilt you know) all these, one: as for the other qualities belonging to, or attending on, a Wife, such as fortune, connections education, ... family blood, &c. divide the two remaining degrees among them as you please ...*

Sensible though this joking formula may be, there is also in it a certain naïve egocentricity that puts the burden of a successful marriage on the woman. Jean Armour's bigness of heart extended to mothering his love-child by Anna Park with the comment that 'our Robbie should have had twa wives'.

It was a shrewd as much as generous comment. Burns not only loved women, he was utterly dependent on them. This may explain some of his attraction for them, for often they appear to have mothered him. This was the case with old Mrs Dunlop of Dunlop, who frequently burdened Burns with kindly advice like some clocking hen. When Burns fell out with Maria Riddell, it was she who made the initial move to reconciliation, even though he as the older of the two had behaved like a petted child in the interval. Perhaps a woman's instinctive understanding of Burns's immaturity in this respect was disarming, and the lack of self-understanding the irritant grit which makes the pearl.

Not all Burns's girlfriends were so easily relieved of their predicament as Anna Park when they found themselves with child. On balance it seems that the erotic tension between 'Sylvander' and 'Clarinda' – Burns and Nancy McLehose – was not consummated. Burns's physical head of steam was relieved in the person of Jenny Clow, Clarinda's servant lass. He also may have *bairn't* May Cameron, another servant girl in Edinburgh, although it may have been a false alarm, or a miscarriage ensued. Although he was willing to take Jenny Clow's child into his own household, it was symptomatic of a different and split world, where physical satisfaction was in one place and emotional fulfilment was in another. It also raises the tension between emotional and intellectual fulfilment in Burns's life on which people have often speculated.

The Peggy Chalmers to whom Burns wrote describing Jean is the other woman whom the posthumous matchmakers have had in mind for him, and 'Clarinda' cattily suggested that at the time. There is no doubt that their minds met, and had Peggy not been betrothed to another when Burns proposed to her, it is a matter of speculation as to whether she might have accepted. (She would not have divulged his proposal years later had she not been moved by it.) Her refusal did not break their friendship, the real test of their mutual understanding. Here was someone who united both physical and intellectual attraction, and Burns could acknowledge this to her later with remarkable directness. He wrote to her on 16 September 1788, reflecting on time spent together, that he had 'lived more of a real life with you in eight days, than I can do with almost anybody I meet with in eight years – when I think on the improbability of meeting you in this world again – I could sit down and cry like a child!'.

Margaret Chalmers, Mrs Lewis Hay (1783?–1843), by John Irvine. Had she not been betrothed already when Burns proposed marriage to her in 1787, his subsequent life might have been very different.

Yet there was one divide between them. It was not one of 'manners' or of education, but the practical one which related to livelihoods. All the advice Burns had had since his rise to fame pointed him back to the land and its people as the source of his inspiration. His patrons liked the idea of their ploughman-poet, and that in the first instance was what he chose. Some of this is revealed in a letter Burns wrote to Mrs Dunlop on 10 August 1788. In discussing his recent marriage to Jean Armour, beneath the aureate phrases several interesting points tumble out: 'I could never have got a female partner for life who could have entered into my favorite studies, relished my favorite Authors, &c. without entailing on me at the same time, expensive living, fantastic caprice, apish affectation ... ' All this despite the possible prospect of employment in the Excise, which 'poor as it may *comparatively* be, whose emoluments are luxury to any thing my first twenty five years of Life could promise'. Already he hints that the farm at Ellisland may turn out to be, in his familiar phrase, 'a ruinous bargain'. Yet he was going to have a good shot at it. In preparation, Jean is 'regularly & constantly apprentice to my Mother & Sisters in their dairy & other rural business'.

There was good reason for this. In the farming economy of the south west of that day, the *guidwife* was as vital as the farmer. The making of cheese, a long and time-consuming business, paid a substantial portion of the rent. It also took a lot of skill. In the absence of scientific knowledge, success depended on experience gathered over years, and the small-town-bred Jean was undergoing a crash course in just that at the hands of Rob-

Bogjurgan, in the Braes of Glenbervie. Robert Burns's great-great grandfather Walter
Burnes (d. 1670) once farmed here. This area was strongly Episcopalian until after the
Jacobite Rising of 1745. Robert's father, William, was an orthodox Calvinist in doctrine,
but his more liberal attitude and intellect may owe something to his North-East
background.
Photo: Gavin Sprott

Frances Anna
Wallace, Mrs Dunlop
of Dunlop (1730–
1815). From 1786
onwards, Burns and
Mrs Dunlop
corresponded
regularly for more
than eight years, until
they fell out over
events in
Revolutionary
France. A letter of
reconciliation reached
Burns on his
deathbed.
Reproduced from *The
Land of Burns.*

ert's family. She grew fond of her cows at Ellisland, but whether she ever made much of a success of her cheese-making is not known. If this contributed to the financial difficulties of Ellisland, Burns did not mention it. The simple fact is that, he had had enough of farming.

It is sometimes suggested that, in marrying Jean Armour, Burns denied himself a helpmeet who was a true kindred spirit. Jean was evidently free of affectation, loved her husband dearly and got on with life. In settling with Jean, Burns chose not some 'simple life', but a world that they shared. She, as much as her husband, had defied the hatchet-faced rigidity of Calvinist orthodoxy with her 'sprightly cheerfulness'; she had been an equal participant in the joys of the flesh; and in the practicalities of family life she showed a sober decency. As he remembered his mother's singing, so Burns took great pleasure in Jean's 'wood-notes wild'. As we shall see, Burns saw in that combination of word and song the essential spirit of Scotland. The old songs included a morality that was often elusive and inconsistent, sometimes harsh, but that also embodied the wisdom of ages.

CHAPTER FOUR

WORD AND SONG

In 1563 one Ninian Winyet left Scotland never to return. He was one of the conservative kirkmen who refused to accept the Reformation that had taken place three years before, and the most articulate critic of the new order. He is now remembered not by his learned tracts but by the parting squib he cast at John Knox in an open letter:

> *Gif ye, throw curiositie of novationis, hes foryet our auld plane Scottis quhilk your mother leirit you, in tymes cuming I shall wryte to you my mind in Latin, for I am nocht acquayntit with your Southeroun.*

Indeed, Knox had plenty of occasion to practise his English. While the Reformation was still brewing up in Scotland, he had spent four years in England and, on and off, six years ministering to English congregations at Frankfurt-am-Main and Geneva. He was one of six chaplains to Edward VI of England. When the Reformation in Scotland was threatened by the French in 1560, it was mainly Knox who enlisted English help to defeat them. His first wife was English, and he sent his two sons by that marriage to England for their education. When he came to write his comprehensive *History of the Reformation in Scotland*, he wrote it in English.

The Bibles that Knox and his fellow reformers used were in English, as was *The Book of Common Order*, and their manifesto, the *First Book of Discipline*. The only complete translation of the New Testament into Scots was by Murdoch Nisbet, done in secret about 1520 in the days of James V. It was not published until 1901, and then as an antiquarian curiosity. The God of the Reformation thus spoke in English.

This was to have far-reaching effects. Coupled with the removal of king and court to England on the Union of the Crowns in 1603, Scots declined as the language of officialdom and literary expression. Yet all is not as simple as it seems.

The English version of the Bible which became the standard for over three centuries was produced in 1611 at the behest of the first British monarch, James VI. It was the work of several scholars, and their intention was direct and practical: to make the scriptures available to all. Thus it was rendered into a straightforward English that makes no concession to ornament or linguistic subtlety. This is borne out in the vocabulary. It uses only a quarter of the words found in Shakespeare. The language does not have that quality that Shakespeare bequeathed to modern English, where words develop a sinuous and almost athletic character, the smallest shades of meaning identified by an ever-expanding vocabulary conscripted from a wide range of sources. The linguistic beauty of the King James Bible comes from another tradition. It has the simplicity and force of a ballad, reproducing that character of ballads and sagas, where the running water of innumerable tongues has smoothed not just the outer shape but the inner dynamics, reflecting both ancient wisdom and prejudice, and in that it is true to the original. The most substantial Scots prose work of modern times, Lorimer's New Testament, reproduces the cadences of the King James Bible, not because it was translated from it (he worked from the oldest texts) but because it is in a common linguistic tradition.

If Holy Writ thus came in English, it was not just because of the anglophile tendencies of the reformers, but because, for all the linguistic difference, it could be understood. For the reformers in both countries, biblical English was not in the first instance a cultural but a spiritual language. It would have varied quite markedly from the regional dialects commonly spoken over large parts of England well into the nineteenth century, as well as Scots, but as long as people could work out the message, that was all that mattered.

This drive to open the Scriptures to the people had far-reaching consequences, and in England some clerics later had cause to regret it, for here was a rod the reformed church had made for the backs of its own clergy. With the zeal for mastering detail that often characterises the self-taught, ordinary people began to dig into what was now their possession. Now everybody was reading from the same script, and when they could not agree on what they found, especially as they were concerned with Holy Writ, there were the seeds of an explosive situation that would be played out in the following century.

In Scotland the old pre-Reformation Kirk was top-heavy with civilised, often learned and often worldly, prelates and other office holders. The top

A
NEW EDITION
OF THE
LIFE
AND
HEROICK ACTIONS
OF THE RENOUN'D
Sir *William Wallace,*
GENERAL and GOVERNOUR
OF
SCOTLAND.

Wherein the Old obsolete Words are rendered more Intelligible; and adapted to the understanding of such who have not leisure to study the Meaning, and Import of such Phrases without the help of a Glossary.

GLASGOW,
Printed by WILLIAM DUNCAN
M. DCC. XXII.

Frontispiece to a 1722 Glasgow edition of Henry the Minstrel's *Life and Heroick Actions of Sir William Wallace,* abridged by William Hamilton of Gilbertfield. In his letter of 2 August 1787 Burns told Dr Moore: 'The first two books I ever read in private, and which gave me more pleasure than any two books I ever read again, were the life of Hannibal and the history of Sir William Wallace'.

offices were fat and grand enough to offer a worthwhile career for the younger sons of the nobility, but the price was a huge neglect of the parish ministry, because the money that was there to support the parish kirks was frequently diverted to keep up the great abbeys and cathedrals and their officials. The reformers were determined that 'The Word' should never again be stranded in the care of a remote elite. An educated ministry and instructed congregations were central to the vision of the reformed Kirk at the outset. The bigger Burghs were already served with schools dating from before the Reformation. Schools began to appear in country parishes, and in 1611 the Privy Council issued the first formal instruction that one be set up in every parish, to be paid for by the local *heritors* or landowners, and charging modest fees from the scholars' parents. Although this vision was approaching practical reality in the Lowlands within half a century, it was far from the whole story. Many such schools were inaccessible in large country parishes, but by the eighteenth century such was the interest in education that they were supplemented by many small, private ventures. By the time that Burns was born, the level of literacy in the Lowland Scottish countryside was probably the highest in Europe, and only paralleled in parts of England, fuelled by a similar devotional interest in the Bible.

As we have seen, people were learning to read a lean, laconic English that was closely akin to Scots in character. Centuries later this would surface in the most surprising places. Lewis Grassic Gibbon's *Sunset Song* (1932) is written in English, but behind it are the cadences of the Scots tongue, and also a lyrical quality reminiscent of that old biblical English. The rhythmic balance of the descriptive passages, the cool directness and the accurate use of simple words are what give the writing such force.

The written language of Sir Walter Scott is very different from the old biblical English, and thus also from Scots. It has elegance rather than beauty, and is built on the legacy of Augustan English established in the seventeenth century and current in the eighteenth. It has an expanding vocabulary with an omnivorous appetite, so that there is a precise word to distinguish even the smallest shade of meaning. In the eighteenth century the spheres of literature, science and philosophy were growing at a quite extraordinary rate, and even then English was one of the main languages in which that information was accessible. The ability to speak as well as write English was a sign of intellectual advancement. Access to knowledge and understanding is also why Burns acquired a reading knowledge of French, as the main rival of English in philosophy and science. John Murdoch, whom William Burnes and his neighbours had engaged to teach their children in Alloway, went on to become a teacher of French in London. William Smellie, one of Burns's closest Edinburgh friends, himself the son of a stone-mason, became the first editor of the *Encyclopaedia Britannica* in 1771. Although Smellie could not pronounce a word of French, he translated it competently. The other language of intellectual communication was Latin, but by now that star was fading. Maria Riddell, an educated woman who became one of Burns's principal friends in Dumfriesshire, realised that with his mental ability he could easily have learned Latin, and once she asked him why he did not do so. In fact, Burns was acquainted with many of the classical authors through English translations, but his reply to her was that 'he knew all the Latin that he desired to learn, and that was *omnia vincit amor*'.

Yet whatever the utility of various languages for conveying information, sooner or later there will be consequences when an incoming language does not merely communicate, but starts to invade. From the early eighteenth century a serious split in the spoken as well as the written language was becoming apparent in Scotland. This split would become social as well as intellectual, but the process still had a long way to go in Burns's day. In his famous review of the first edition of Burns's poems printed in the Edinburgh-based *Lounger* magazine, Henry Mackenzie expressed a fear that soon people would not be able to understand these wonderful poems because they were written in some fading rural *patois*. Of course, who he meant by 'people' is open to question. Perhaps he had no notion as to the enduring reception that the poems would receive from *the* people.

Henry Dundas was a major figure of the British political establishment, and because of his power and influence he was in effect the un-crowned king of Scotland. He made no attempt to dilute his Scottishness. Scott, who lived half a generation after Burns, a man of broad learning and with a reading knowledge of several European tongues, spoke Scots as readily as English. Lord Cockburn, yet another generation on, bred of the Edinburgh *haute bourgeoisie*, spoke Scots as well as English. Much has been made of the terror the late eighteenth-century educated Scots, including for instance David Hume, had of committing Scotticisms. James Boswell was in the vanguard of Scots gentry sending their children for an English education, yet his son Alexander printed a volume of vigorous poems in

Allan Ramsay senior
(1686–1758),
sketched in 1729 by
his son Allan. The
Tea-Table Miscellany,
or collection of songs,
brought out (in four
volumes, between
1724 and 1737) by
wig-maker, bookseller
and poet Ramsay,
captivated public
taste with its skilful
arrangements of
traditional Scottish
lyrics and airs. Its
popularity
undoubtedly shaped
Burns's approach to
songwriting.

the Ayrshire tongue, contributed to George Thomson's *A Select Collection of Scotish Airs*, and was largely responsible for erecting the Alloway monument to the memory of Burns. This fear of Scotticisms has perhaps been exaggerated and misunderstood. The fear was not necessarily of Scots itself, but the *gaucherie* of conflating Scots and English, the equivalent blunder of a cultured man not knowing his Latin grammar. Looking back from the next century, Carlyle identified the writing of eighteenth-century Scotland, indeed Britain, as being cosmopolitan, 'without any local environment'. If there was any cast of character to Scottish writing, it was an interest in French rather than English ideas. For the Scottish sages of the Enlightenment, 'the field of their life shows neither briers nor roses: but only a flat, continuous threshing floor for Logic'. The religionists had Thomas Boston's *Fourfold State of Man* (1720), the intellectuals had David Hume's *Enquiry Concerning Human Understanding* (1748), the political economists had Adam Smith's *Inquiry into the Nature and Causes of the Wealth of Nations* (1776).

Others had ploughed the vernacular furrow before Burns. In particular he acknowledged 'Honest Allan' Ramsay and Robert Fergusson with fulsome praise, erecting a proper memorial to the latter in the Canongate kirkyard at some considerable expense to himself. Yet people immediately recognised that Burns was a giant in comparison, reaching far beyond the humorous and charming pastorale of Ramsay's *The Gentle Shepherd* or the muscular satire of Fergusson's *Leith Races*.

Burns burst in on late eighteenth-century Scotland with a language which was remarkable then not for some Scottishness, but for its balance and directness. The frontier of elegance and aureate delicacy as expressed in Augustan English was pushed back to where people felt it belonged. Nor was it just that the language spoke from the heart. The leaven of intellect was working in it as well. 'To a Mouse' is justly famed for catching that mood of introspection and foreboding that sometimes gripped the poet. The mastery of language appears effortless and is sublime. Yet there is a philosophical keel to the work. At the beginning man and mouse may be divided, but they are part of the same creation:

I'm truly sorry man's dominion
Has broken Nature's social union,
An justifies that ill opinion,
Which makes thee startle,
At me, thy poor, earth-born companion,
An fellow-mortal!

But at the end, he puts his finger on the dynamics of human as opposed to animal feelings:

Still thou art blest, compar'd wi me!
The present only toucheth thee …

If Gilbert Burns, Gavin Hamilton and others encouraged Burns to get his poems published in Kilmarnock, it was the Edinburgh literati who pushed him towards a national publication. They were responding to a language and idiom they understood only too well.

As we shall see, Robert Heron's *Memoir* of Burns, the first semblance of a biography to be published after the poet's death, was so riddled with inaccuracy that it is rash to rely on anything he said. Nevertheless, one comment is of interest: 'I can well remember, how that even plough-boys and maid-servants would have gladly bestowed the wages which they earned the most hardly, and which they wanted to purchase necessary clothing, if they might but procure the works of Burns'. What we might deduce is that whether these plough-boys and maid-servants did or did not want to get hold of Burns's poems, it would not have been out of character if they did. Burns and literacy went together. It was through literacy that the poems were in circulation before any collected publication. Some of the satires such as 'Holy Willie's Prayer' circulated as broadsheets. Burns copied out others for interested parties, and they achieved a kind of samizdat currency. Relatively few would have been able to afford the first Kilmarnock 1786 printing even if they could have got their hands on it. It cost three shillings, which for most people was at least two or three weeks' in-

Robert Fergusson (1750–74) by Alexander Runciman. Burns was disgusted that a brother poet should have died so young, in debt and in a mad-house. He petitioned for a headstone to be erected, at his expense, on Fergusson's grave in the Canongate kirkyard.

75

Title page and
frontispiece of *The
Works in Verse and
Prose of William
Shenstone.*
The young Burns was
an avid reader of
Milton, Pope, and
The Spectator, before
moving on to the
nature poetry of
London-based fellow
Scot James Thomson,
and the English
gentleman-amateur,
William Shenstone.
He modelled his style
of writing English on
these various sources.
This 'Augustan'
English varied from
flowery politeness to
a skilful directness.

NATIONAL LIBRARY OF
SCOTLAND

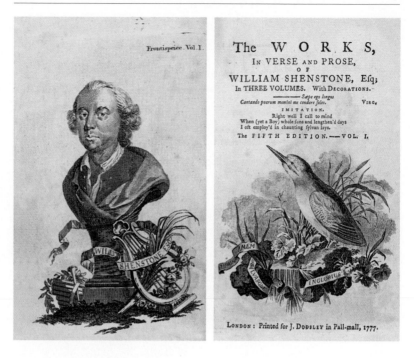

come, and only about six hundred copies were printed, and within a month
they were all gone. Yet within a few years the printers could not turn the
books out fast enough.

The improved printing technology of the 1820s came in time to benefit
Scott, but it further expanded the sale of Burns. The combination of literacy
and a busy publishing industry meant that Burns became built into the
native culture of Lowland Scotland at a time of far-reaching structural
change. The works of Burns would take their place beside the Bible, and
stay there — after Blind Harry's *Wallace* had long been laid aside — and
not just in a *bole* or recess by the *ingle neuk* of a rural cotter house, but on a
shelf in the city tenement.

It is significant that the most vigorous continuation of the old, anonymous, non-book culture of native Lowland ballad and song would be at the
opposite end of the Lowlands, in the north east of Scotland, in what was
still that old Europe of small peasant farmers so wonderfully portrayed in
William Alexander's *Johnny Gibb of Gushetneuk* (1871). Although he could
not foresee it, Burns got on to a different kind of track in which the native
tradition would continue, but changed, living in the blood-stream of the
industrial Scotland that lay ahead, much of it contained between the covers
of a book, and first coming to life in the mind of a reader. Yes, the songs

would be sung in countless Burns Clubs, church so-
cials and in Caledonian societies across the world,
but out of a book or off a printed sheet of music,
most likely arranged for a keyboard accompaniment.

Burns had not built up his formidable range
of reading and store of native songs and ballads for
nothing. His careful and intelligent craftsmanship
has been ably demonstrated by critics and scholars
from Thomas Carlyle to David Daiches, Thomas
Crawford, Donald Low and others. Yet that was not
how it appeared at the time. Many of the literati
imagined that he had been visited by a muse in an
immaculate conception of artless genius, and that
he was a kind of miracle, taking Burns at his word in
his description of the muse Coila in 'The Vision':

> 'And wear thou this' – She solemn said,
> And bound the holly round my head:
> The polish'd leaves and berries red
> Did rustling play;
> And, like a passing thought, she fled
> In light away.

Title page to volume
one of James
Johnson's *The Scots
Musical Museum*, first
published in 1787.
Burns was the major
contributor to the
next four volumes of
the six-part set. Just
weeks before his own
death Burns wrote to
Johnson: 'I will
venture to prophesy,
that to future ages
your Publication will
be the text book &
standard of Scotish
Song & Music'.

But the converse was also apparent among ordinary people. Burns
spoke in their language. If they could master metre and rhyme, they too
could be poets. One of Burns's great supporters among the Ayrshire gentry
was Mrs Dunlop of Dunlop. A traditionalist living in the country, she probably spoke as much Scots as English. A kindly old fusser, she had character,
but was not possessed of anything like a startling intellect. When she sent
Burns some verse written by one of her maids, imagining that she had
discovered a prodigy, the poet groaned. One consequence of his success
was that the old balladry would be driven into the shade by an uncritical
imitation of his own verse. Indeed, this would have been reinforced by the
fact that the notion of verse divorced from song would have seemed quite
novel to country people. Blind Harry's *Wallace* would have been seen as a
story rather than a poem. Tuneless verse was for town-educated gentry.

This was not the case with song. If anything there was a kind of re-
versal, in that the gentry looked to a tradition of native song, to pastoral
poetry as a reminder of their own roots and identity, because they not only
knew the old songs and sang them, but also devised new ones. Song was a

Stock-and-horn. This shows the simple instrument being played. The few surviving examples of the instrument are elaborate antiquaries' versions.

NATIONAL MUSEUM OF SCOTLAND

normal form of expression, a natural extension of speech, not the party or concert piece of the modern folk singer. People sang as some still whistle, going about their everyday business. They sang as they reaped, they sang as they milked the cattle and, also in those days, the sheep, to sooth the animals and help them to let their milk down. As Jane Elliot wrote:

> *I've heard the lilting at our yowe milking*
> *Lasses a-lilting before the dawn o' day.*
>
> THE FLOWERS OF THE FOREST

Other songs were to relieve boredom. The endless treadmill of spinning *lint* or flax into yarn is reflected in the jingle:

> *The weary pund, the weary pund,*
> *The weary pund o tow!*
> *I think my wife will end her life*
> *Before she spin her tow*
>
> THE WEARY PUND O' TOW

Probably the commonest use to which song was put was the lullaby. Thus people absorbed song with their mother's milk, and with it their attitude to life. That was so in Burns's case, for he recalled his mother's songs. Other such songs he later noted on his travels. He first heard 'Ca' the Yowes' from John Clunie, a kirk *precentor* or leader in song. Some verses he added himself, others he 'mended'. It is a simple reflective love-song, and Burns's earlier version probably lies closest to the original:

> *As I gaed down the water-side,*
> *There I met my shepherd lad:*
> *He row'd me sweetly in his plaid,*
> *An he ca'd me his dearie*

> *'Ye sall get gowns and ribbons meet,*
> *Cauf-leather shoon upon your feet,*
> *And in my arms thou'lt lie and sleep,*
> *An ye sall be my dearie'.*

78

It is hard to imagine that this lovely thing would not have been sung as a cradle-song. The slow lilt rising to a lingering note at the end of each verse complements the words perfectly. Here word and melody are part of a seamless garment, and the achievement lies partly in Burns's method. Unlike the great German *Lieder,* the songs were not reared on the poetry, but often both were devised in parallel and shaken down together, or the words formed in the shadow of a tune whose architecture suited Burns's purpose. Such is 'the song I composed out of compliment to Mrs Burns', 'Of A' the Airts the Wind Can Blaw', a free and blithesome song to William Marshall's 'Miss Admiral Gordon's Strathspey', where the two verses play out the exact extent of the composition, and the syllables at the end of every second line match the snap of the music, but also the vital word 'Jean' at the end of each verse.

The sweet, reedy sound of the Lowland pipes would still have been familiar in Burns's day.

NATIONAL MUSEUMS OF SCOTLAND

Thus Burns was always on the hunt for musical as much as poetic inspiration. Coupled with this was the keen historical interest of an ethnomusicologist. In his letter of 19 November 1794 to George Thomson, his Edinburgh musical collaborator, we hear his shout of triumph on discovering a stock-and-horn: 'I have, *at last,* gotten one,' and he then proceeds to give a precise description, both for Thomson's interest and to relay to the artist David Allan so that he could produce an accurate image of the instrument. We do not know if Burns ever heard the stock-and-horn played, but it is probable that he did not.

However, there was another musical tradition that was vanishing in the Lowlands which may have pulled at Burns's heart in a very personal way, because he would have identified it with his father, and that was the singing of the Psalms. Before the 'Second Reformation' wrought its final destruction in the 1640s, the reformed Kirk had established a considerable repertoire of psalm settings for unaccompanied voice but with different parts, and the singing was taught in Burgh schools. Under the latter-day reformers the Psalms were reduced to a standard common metre and the teaching of the old settings died away, and so the musicianship and many of the old tunes were lost. The Psalms were in effect abandoned to the people but with an interesting result. A new demotic tradition took over in which the *precentor* led off the singing and the congregation followed half a line behind. The boxed-in metre was relentlessly stretched into a long, sustained chant. From the mid-eighteenth century Lowland Scotland began to turn its back on what was now something old-fashioned with the import of hymns and modern tunes from the south, and in Episcopal chapels, even, that *kist o' whistles,* the organ. But the old tradition would have been

One of Allan Ramsay's *Scots Songs* (Edinburgh, 1719). The lyric is remarkably similar to that of 'Auld Lang Syne'. Like other great artists, Burns had no hesitation about setting his genius to work on borrowed materials.

NATIONAL LIBRARY OF SCOTLAND

[13]

❀❀❀❀❀❀❀❀❀❀❀❀❀❀❀❀❀❀❀❀❀❀

The Kind Reception,

To the Tune of Auld lang fyne.

I.

SHOULD auld Acquaintance be forgot,
   tho' they return with Scars?
Thefe are the noble HEROE's Lot,
   obtain'd in glorious Wars:
Welcome my FARO to my Breaſt,
   thy Arms about me twine,
And make me once again as bleſt,
   as I was lang fyne.

II.

Methinks around us on each Bough
   a Thouſand Cupids play,
Whilſt thro' the Groves I walk with you
   each Object makes me gay.
Since your Return the Sun and Moon
   with brighter Beams do ſhine,'
Streams murmure ſoft Notes while they run,
   as they did lang fyne.

C   III. De:

Niel Gow (1727–
1807) painted by Sir
Henry Raeburn in
1787. Burns met the
well-known composer
and violinist at
Dunkeld in August of
that year, and later set
many lyrics to dance
tunes by Gow.

SCOTTISH NATIONAL PORTRAIT
GALLERY

William Marshall's
fiddle. Burns greatly
admired Marshall's
springs or airs, and
his strathspeys.

EDINBURGH UNIVERSITY
COLLECTION OF HISTORIC
MUSICAL INSTRUMENTS.
PHOTO: SEAN HUDSON

familiar in William Burnes's household, and his son caught
its shadow in words in 'The Cotter's Saturday Night':

> *They chant their artless notes in simple guise,*
> *They tune their hearts, by far the noblest aim:*
> *Perhaps* Dundee's *wild-warbling measures rise,*
> *Or plaintive* Martyrs, *worthy of the name;*
> *Or noble* Elgin *beets the heavenward flame,*
> *The sweetest far of Scotia's holy lays …*

This survives, still accessible in Gaelic services on
the radio, where the unaccompanied singing of the Psalms
is maintained by the Free Church of Scotland. It has an
eerie and arresting other-worldly beauty.

Burns did not seem to have the same feeling for the
Lowland pipes. Although their popularity was much reduced, they were
not on the verge of extinction like the stock-and-horn. Perhaps Burns identified them with the Burghs, which often maintained official pipers, whereas
the stock-and-horn had been the instrument of the country herd, and also
the musical symbol he chose for his seal.

Yet even the Lowland pipes would be pushed into virtual oblivion by
the triumph of the fiddle, which, far from being an object of antiquarian
interest, had over the century developed with great vigour, creating its own
permanent record as it progressed. It is an interesting fact that the first
printed versions of Scots tunes appeared in England, in John Playford's *The
English Dancing Master* of 1650. From that time on 'Scotch tunes' became
a popular export. Until then, the six-stringed viol had been the instrument
of 'art' music, and the old crude *fithel* the popular, stringed instrument.
Now both were shouldered out by the four-stringed Italian violin and its
German derivatives, with its back as well as its top carved into the shape
that served to create the incisive and sparkling tone. The Italian violin was
becoming available on the return of Charles II in 1660, and in the following century there grew a native skill in making fine instruments, Matthew
Hardie in particular being remembered as the 'Scottish Stradi-
varius'. The instrument on which the cateran James
Macpherson played his last *rant,* and which he shattered before he was hanged on 16 November 1700, was of the same
kind as that which graced the concerts of Handel and Kelly in
Edinburgh, and of same kind as that with which Niel Gow
entertained Burns, played at grand dances, and on which he

would amuse himself at home playing Corelli sonatas.

What we now recognise in fiddle music as something particularly Scottish in character had its origin in the eighteenth century, partly through this adoption of the violin with all its possibilities. The musical life of Edinburgh was particularly active in 'art' as well as what was then 'popular' music, so the standards of musicianship were high. William McGibbon's *Collection of Scots Tunes, Some with Variations*, which came out in three volumes between 1742 and 1755, established native fiddle music as something that was then modern and 'alive'. Nor was it a specifically Lowland thing. Much of the music was developed in the eastern Highlands, including the new strathspey from the 1760s, in which Burns particularly delighted. The restrictions placed on the Highland pipes as instruments of war following the '45 Rising until 1782 opened the road for the advance of the fiddle across the central Highlands into Skye and Lewis.

However, if there was one *raison d'être* for fiddle music, it was for dancing to, and for Burns this was one of the joys of life, but not without early problems. As he described to Dr Moore in his letter of 2 August 1787: 'In my seventeenth year ... I went to a country dancing school. – My father had an unaccountable antipathy against these meetings; and my going was, what to this hour I repent, in absolute defiance of his commands'. In fact, William Burnes soon gave way to a softer line, allowing other members of the family to go as well, but there was nothing unaccountable in his initial attitude at all. He was merely reflecting the view of conservative orthodoxy

Detail from The Penny Wedding by David Allan. The guests helped to supply and finance the food and drink. Any money left over went to the newly-married couple. Penny weddings got a bad name among the guardians of morality.

NATIONAL GALLERY OF SCOTLAND

then still widely held by the older generation. As Andrew Melville and his fellow travellers began to get a grip on Kirk policy in the late sixteenth century, battle was joined with the populace against the evils of dancing. This reached a high tide in 1649 with the Act of Assembly against dancing. What was thought particularly scandalous was the 'promiscuous [ie mixed] dancing of men with women'. The populace stood the phrase on its head, and prized *promisky* dancing as the most enjoyable. The Kirk was battling with more than just dancing, for that was tied up with wedding celebrations, which involved inbuilt social custom, and within that a kind of ritual disinhibition. So the Kirk had to battle also against the *penny bridal*, where guests and well-wishers all chipped in with ample supplies of food and alcoholic refreshments. Against the Highlands and Islands such edicts were futile, and in the Lowlands it was only a matter of time before they failed. When the Duke and Duchess of York (later King James VII and his queen) stayed at Holyrood House between 1680 and 1682, they re-established dancing in Lowland Scotland as an aristocratic entertainment. By the end of the century the gentry were openly snubbing the Kirk, and early in the following century there were regular public assemblies at the West Bow in Edinburgh, and the example spread to the principal towns. Where they went the common people followed, and by the 1750s the dam was fast crumbling.

This kind of music and dance was the expression of a new and confident sense of freedom, and, because it was *promisky*, sexual freedom. This new sense of liberty also involved drink. We have seen how ale was a normal and nutritious part of the diet, but the widespread distillation of whisky was something new. Burns's crack that 'whisky and freedom gang thegither' was true in an economic as much as a social way. The product was portable and therefore saleable, part of the expanding money economy, and also part of a black market of untaxed goods. Thus dancing, celebrations, and even public events such as the 'holy fairs' in preparation for the communions, were occasions for drink. Drink was part of companionship and social mirth. The joyful spirit is captured in 'Willie Brew'd a Peck o Maut', when Burns and his schoolmaster friends Allan Masterton and William Nicol had a happy reunion at Moffat in 1789:

> *We are na fou, we're nae that fou,*
> *But just a drappie in our e'e!*
> *The cock may crae, the day may daw,*
> *And ay we'll taste the barley bree!*

Nae that fou? Their back teeth were awash! But Burns was always careful to distinguish between dissipation and debauchery. For him the first was harmless indulgence, the second something different, dark and repugnant. Through occasional 'dissipation' he got the odd sore head. Sometimes for dramatic effect he pretended to have been drunk when he hadn't been. Once, when he really was, he managed to make a fool of himself in front of his Riddell friends at Friars' Carse near Ellisland. Here it was a social blunder that he very much regretted, not some moral dimension. It was the social virtue of drink that Burns celebrated in song, not drink itself. Only once does Burns mention turning to the bottle for consolation. Why drink alone when you can drink in company? Solitary tippling was a painful eccentricity, and to people at the time this suggestion was probably the cruellest cut against the alcoholic Willie Fisher in 'Holy Willie's Prayer'.

Besides working the vast social quarry of his experience, Burns would make wide use of manuscript and printed sources for songs that he would work on. He consulted not just Allan Ramsay's collections, but for instance William Thomson's *Orpheus Caledonius* of 1725, and not only David Herd's *Ancient Scottish Songs, Heroic Ballads* of 1769, but also the manuscripts and notes on which they were based, which Herd generously made available to him. But where Herd had built up his information largely by correspondence, Burns was omnivorous. As with the contraband he would later search out as an exciseman, there was little that escaped his vigilant eye, and his hunting ground was the life he saw before him.

Josiah Walker recorded an interesting – and indeed most attractive – eye-witness account of an incident when Burns was in Edinburgh. A friend found his daughter of twelve seated with the poet at a harpsichord. She sang and played an accompaniment which they both adjusted with repeated trials. Burns was totally absorbed. It was a pattern for the partnership that Burns would need in the future.

This absorption in collecting and 'mending' old songs was to become the dominant interest in the later part of Burns's life. However, once he envisaged making a systematic publication, he ventured on to different territory. He could sing, he could play the fiddle after a fashion, he could recognise a good tune when he heard one, but he never laid any claim to proficient musicianship. Yet he had one vital skill: he could record music. In this aspect he was in total contrast to Scott, who boasted that 'no man in Britain had more songs by heart than I could have mustered'. Yet when he published his *Minstrelsy of the Scottish Border* in 1802, Scott did not include one tune. Burns admitted forgetting interesting tunes that he had failed to

Writing about some of 'the old pieces that are still to be found among our Peasantry in the West', Burns was being less than candid when, in August 1787, he informed the antiquarian, William Tytler of Woodhouselee: 'I invariably hold it sacriledge to add any thing of my own to help out with the shatter'd wrecks of these venerable old compositions'. In fact, Burns was to amend lyrics and swap airs as freely as Ramsay had done before him.

NATIONAL LIBRARY OF SCOTLAND: MS.586.

record, and regretted it. On the other hand, some regretted the very process of recording old songs. In his *Domestic Manners and Private Life of Sir Walter Scott* of 1834, James Hogg ('The Ettrick Shepherd') recalls a terrific telling-off his mother, Margaret Laidlaw, gave Scott:

> There war never ane o' my sangs prentit till ye prentit them yoursel', an' ye hae spoilt them awthegither. They were made for singin' an' no for readin'; but ye hae broken the charm noo, an' they'll never [be] sung mair. An' the worst thing of a' they're nouther richt spell'd nor richt setten down.

This was just the perilous course that Burns was about to embark on, but with the inclusion of the tunes. To further this project he required a collaborator. In the event he found more than one, or rather they found him. The first was James Johnson, a Borderer seventeen years older than himself who had settled in Edinburgh. He was an engraver specialising in printing and selling music, and when Burns met him in Edinburgh he was already about to publish the first volume of his *Scots Musical Museum*. 'Museum' did not then have its modern connotation of an antiquaries' zoo, but signified the home of the Muses, that is, of inspiration. The next four volumes were largely filled with work collected and worked on by Burns. And here was this very process of codifying and institutionalising the songs for onward transmission into a different world. Stephen Clarke, a musician and organist, rendered the tunes into a keyboard setting. And significantly, for the tunes themselves, Burns allowed himself a much wider range, conscripting them from beyond his native Lowlands.

In James Johnson, Burns had a kindred spirit with an ear attuned to the traditional music, and whose judgement coincided with his own. Johnson was also mild-mannered and lacked the confidence of much education to interfere with Burns's opinion. As Burns wrote to him in June 1796, aware that he was a dying man:

> Many a merry meeting this Publication has given us … Your Work is a great one; & though, now that it is near finished, I see if we were to begin again, two or three things that might be mended, yet I will venture to prophesy, that to future ages your Publication will be the text book & standard of Scotish Song & Music.

The second main collaborator, George Thomson, was a different man with a different aim. The son of a Fife dominie, two years older than Burns, he was a middle-ranking civil servant in Edinburgh and an able amateur

George Thomson (1757–1851), drawn by William Nicholson *c.* 1817. Whereas James Johnson largely entrusted his project to Burns's judgement, Thomson, who was an educated man, was conceited enough to consider his own taste at least as good as Burns's, and occasionally altered the poet's lyrics for the press without telling him.

classical musician. In 1792 he wrote to Burns asking him to supply the raw material of songs for inclusion in his *Select Collection of Scotish Airs*. The foremost composers of the day would then arrange these songs, complete with instrumental introduction and conclusion. Haydn, Beethoven, Pleyel, Kozeluch and Hummel were involved. Although their settings have sometimes been miscalled as taking Burns quite out of the native idiom, that is rash. Thomson wanted the songs to figure in the mainstream of European vocal music.

Although a competent musician and an educated man, Thomson's understanding of poetry was limited to a dogged orthodoxy. Having drawn Burns into his project, and with the poet's cheerful assurance that he would defer to his opinion, he was to discover the path a more arduous one than he had perhaps bargained for. Burns never lost patience, but horse-traded one point for another concession in a long and voluminous correspondence, patiently giving good reason as he went. Burns took the trouble, for as he said in his letter of 7 April 1793:

> *You cannot imagine how much this business of composing for your publication has added to my enjoyments. – What with my early attachment to ballads, Johnson's Museum, your book; &c. Ballad making is now as compleatly my hobby-horse, as ever Fortification was Uncle Toby's …*

Thomson's frequent proposals to meddle with the words have just as frequently irritated Burns's biographers, but the poet was usually able to look after himself. Thomson did not so much offend but invite a challenge. Because Burns respected Thomson as a musician, he felt free to defend his own ground with a good-humoured bluntness. In another letter of April 1793 he wrote to Thomson:

> *Give me leave to criticise your taste in the only thing in which it is in my opinion reprehensible: (you know I ought to know something of my own trade) of pathos, Sentiment & Point, you are a compleat judge; but there is a quality more necessary than either, in a Song, & which is the very essence of a Ballad, I mean Simplicity – now, if I mistake not, this last feature you are a little apt to sacrifice to the foregoing.*

Sometimes Burns would halt Thomson point-blank, as in a letter which Thomson received about 30 June 1793: 'I cannot alter the disputed line, in the Mill Mill! O. – What you think a defect, I esteem as a positive beauty; so you see how Doctors differ'. On other occasions Burns was ruthlessly critical of himself. The following month he wrote: 'The old Ballad, I wish I were where Helen Lies – is silly, to contemptibility. – My alteration of it in Johnson is not much better'.

In the course of fifty-six letters Burns revealed how carefully he worked at his craft and the relationship of word and song. On 8 November 1792 he wrote:

If you mean, my dear Sir, that all the Songs in your Collection shall be poetry of the first merit, I am afraid you will find difficulty in the undertaking more than you are aware of. – There is a peculiar rhythmus in many of our airs, a necessity of adapting syllables to the emphasis, or what I would call the feature notes, *of the tune, that cramps the Poet, & lays him under almost insuperable difficulties.*

He went on to give examples, complete with musical notation. In September 1793, half-laughing at himself, Burns drew this self-portrait:

My way is: I consider the poetic Sentiment, correspondent to my idea of the musical expression; then chuse my theme; begin one Stanza; when that is composed, which is generally the most difficult part of the business, I walk out, sit down now & then, look out for objects in Nature around me that are in unison or harmony with the cogitations of my fancy & workings of my bosom; humming every now & then the air with the verses I have framed: when I feel my Muse beginning to jade, I retire to the solitary fireside of my study, & there commit my effusions to paper; swinging, at intervals, on the hind-legs of my elbow-chair, by way of calling forth my own critical strictures, as my pen goes on. – Seriously, this, at home, is almost invariably my way. – What damn'd Egotism!

This reveals a man in command of his own artistic abilities, and at ease with them. When Burns marched his muse towards the sound of political conflict, there would be less ease for him – and others.

'Auld Lang Syne'. A copy of Johnson's *Museum*, with Burns's alterations interleaved.
It was prepared for Burns's friend Robert Riddell.

BURNS COTTAGE & MUSEUM, ALLOWAY

Opposite:
Looking down the Cluden Water to the ruins of Lincluden Abbey, near Dumfries.
Running water was always an inspiration to Burns and here he composed his final version
of 'Ca' the Yowes to the Knowes'.

Hark, the mavis e'ening sang
  Sounding Clouden's woods amang
Then a-faulding let us gang
  My bonnie dearie.

PHOTO: GAVIN SPROTT

CHAPTER FIVE

REVOLUTION

❖❖❖❖❖❖❖❖❖❖❖·❖❖·❖❖❖❖·❖❖❖
❖❖❖❖❖❖❖❖❖❖·❖❖·❖❖❖❖·❖❖❖

When Burns arrived in Edinburgh, he attracted intense interest as a prodigy. This was partly because Henry Mackenzie's review of the Kilmarnock edition of the poems had appeared only a few days before in the December 1786 number of *The Lounger*, a periodical which he edited, and which was popular among the reading public of the capital and beyond. Although he wrote *The Man of Feeling* (1771), Mackenzie's main livelihood was the law, but besides other less successful books he continued in a line of literary journalism. Much of it was dull, hobbled by an almost neurotic fetish with polish and propriety. Burns's Kilmarnock poems seem to have woken him up. The phrase he coined to described Burns, and which has stuck, was 'this Heaven-taught Ploughman'. Perhaps mindful of the moral contained in Gray's *Elegy* (1751), that of the unrealised potential in obscure country people, Mackenzie tackled this point head on:

> *In the discovery of talents generally unknown, men are apt to indulge the same fond partiality as in all other discoveries which themselves have made; and hence we have had repeated instances of painters and of poets, who have been drawn from obscure situations, and held forth to public notice ... yet in a short time have sunk again to their former obscurity.*

Mackenzie's conclusion was that Burns did transcend this limitation, and that he was indeed a remarkable poet. This was not unflattering to himself, as Burn's poems bore all the marks of 'sensibility', of which Mackenzie considered himself to be the great proponent. In a day or two after the *Lounger* review, Mackenzie was to be further flattered by the poet's personal avowal that he treasured *The Man of Feeling* next to the Bible. In

Far left :
Henry Mackenzie
(1745–1831) by
Samuel Joseph.
Mackenzie wrote *The
Man of Feeling,* a
novel which Burns
admired. Mackenzie
eased Burns's path
into the capital's
society by his praise
of the Kilmarnock
edition of his poems.
SCOTTISH NATIONAL PORTRAIT
GALLERY

Left :
William Creech
(1745-1815) painted
by Sir Henry
Raeburn, *c.* 1806.
When, under the
auspices of Henry
Mackenzie, Burns
signed a
memorandum of
agreement with
Creech in April 1787,
he noted the
Edinburgh publisher's
'extreme vanity and
something of the
more harmless
modifications of
selfishness', but was
nonetheless
exasperated when
Creech kept him
waiting almost a year
for the sums
promised.
SCOTTISH NATIONAL PORTRAIT
GALLERY

Mackenzie's book, sensibility might make better people, but not a better world. Harley, Mackenzie's hero, left the world in the same mess as he found it. At that point it never crossed Mackenzie's or anyone else's mind that the ploughman-poet would be interested in doing anything different.

Part of the reason was that the notion of progress was still something to get used to, and to a previous generation it would have seemed foreign. Hitherto, change had not been identified with economics. History was furnished with rattling stories of revolutions and upheavals in plenty, the rise and fall of great empires, but they were pictured in terms of the eternal battle between good and evil, or civilisation and barbarism. The Reformation and the 'Glorious Revolution' of 1688–9 and Scotland's Claim of Right of 1690 were not initially seen as progress, but the reinstatement of lost virtue.

In Burns's day, this picture of a world that was standing still economically was becoming hard to sustain. It must have seemed to most informed people that better times were on the way. Economic expansion was a reality that affected everyday lives. It was demolishing old livelihoods and creating new ones in a way that had never been experienced before. A growth in wealth that was once measured over generations was now obvious over decades, even less. What was behind this extraordinary phenomenon? Adam Smith was the first person to try and get a handle on the dynamics of economic growth in his *Wealth of Nations* in 1766. He examined what happened when there was economic freedom, how that effected markets, and how it produced a division of labour.

Far from being *laissez-faire*, Smith had a concept of community and

James Cunningham, 14th Earl of Glencairn (1749–91) by an unknown artist. Although a grandee, Glencairn showed Burns great kindness, especially when he first arrived in Edinburgh.

PRIVATE COLLECTION

mutual obligation which included government. He may have been the first modern economist, but in this he was also an heir to a philosophy of social contract that had grown out of Huguenot France, Puritan England, Covenanting Scotland, and the colonies of New England. There would be no avoiding the link between expanding wealth and who ran the country. With wealth came education and with education came social mobility. A social order built on an acceptance of poverty and subordination as the divine order could be challenged by personal histories.

James and Agnes Gairdner were brother and sister who lived in late seventeenth-century Ayr. James had a daughter Isabella, who married Hugh McGuire, a *wright* or joiner, who was also noted as a fiddler, and Agnes married Adam MacRae. Agnes lost her husband early, and had to bring up her son James on her own. She supported herself as a washerwoman. At the age of twelve James left home and went to sea as part of the crew of a merchant ship. Agnes's niece Isabella had four daughters and one son to fend for, but showed great kindness to her widowed aunt. The years passed, nothing was heard of James, and Agnes died. Then an advertisement appeared in the local paper. James had returned, and wished to make contact with members of his family. In the meantime, he had risen in the East India Company Service, first to the command of one of their ships, and finally to be Governor of the Madras Presidency. He was, as one historian put it, 'rich beyond the dreams of avarice'.

In gratitude to his cousin Isabella for the kindness she had shown his mother, James poured his treasure out on her children. The daughters had rich *tochers* or dowries settled on them, and to befit them for a different station in life they were sent to receive an appropriate education. One of these daughters was Elizabeth, and at the time of James's return she was working as a young servant girl in the household of one William Tennant.

William was tenant in the Mains at Brigend of Doon. His eldest son, John, and Isabella's daughter, Elizabeth, both born in 1725, were thus familiar as part of the same household. By the custom of the time they would have eaten at the same table and shared the same pastimes. They were also of the same generation as William Burnes, who was older than John by four years. When William settled in Alloway, he and John Tennant became firm friends, and John was one of the witnesses to the christening of William's son Robert.

With her lady's education, in 1744 Elizabeth married William, the 13th Earl of Glencairn. Part of her *tocher* was the Barony of Ochiltree, and twenty-four years after she had become countess, she offered John Tennant the position of factor. He removed from Laigh Corton to Glenconner, where he was both factor of the estate and tenant farmer. Burns remembered him well as 'guid auld Glen, /The ace an wale of honest men'.

The now Countess Elizabeth had two sons. The second, James, succeeded as the 14th Earl of Glencairn. It was he who showed Burns such unequivocal kindness and support, offering him the hospitality of his house, and the introducing him to his circle of acquaintances in Edinburgh; it was also after him that Burns named his third son. When Glencairn died at the age of forty-two in 1791, Burns was genuinely grief-stricken.

> *'The bridegroom may forget the bride*
> *Was made his wedded wife yestreen;*
> *The monarch may forget the crown*
> *That on his head an hour has been;*
> *The mother may forget the child*
> *That smiles sae sweetly on her knee;*
> *But I'll remember thee, Glencairn,*
> *And a' that thou hast done for me!'*
>
> LAMENT FOR JAMES, EARL OF GLENCAIRN

This is a curious and involved web of circumstance, but an informative one. All the details of Glencairn's antecedents on his mother's side would have been totally familiar to the poet, yet there he was, a belted earl and a representative peer for Scotland in the House of Lords. Glencairn's behaviour towards Burns suggests that he was aware of Burns's knowledge, and that he was not ashamed of it. This circumstance alone was a massive denial that gentry or even nobles were some separate sub-species of the human race with a different tincture of blood. They were of the same clay as everyone else. Here also the composition of the nobility, much less the gentry or the common people, was being altered as the direct result of economic change.

When 'great folks', as Burns often called them, treated him with normal consideration and courtesy, his response was always a warm one. Such behaviour was in step with the obligations that came with wealth and rank. When they presumed on that rank, or ignored him as beneath their notice, nothing was surer to provoke the most intense dislike:

> *I tent less, and want less*
> *Their roomy fire-side;*
> *But hanker, and canker,*
> *To see their cursed pride.*
>
> EPISTLE TO DAVIE

The Inauguration of
Robert Burns as Poet
Laureate of Lodge
Canongate
Kilwinning, 1st
March, 1787, by
Stewart Watson. This
was painted long after
the event at which
Burns was toasted as
'Caledonia's Bard'.
Although this shows
many leading figures
of Scottish society at
the time, some of
those depicted were
not even present.

GRAND LODGE OF SCOTLAND

This attitude gave Burns a certain manner that the members of polite
society noticed at the time. He was never arrogant, yet there was about his
demeanour the hint of a prickly pride that could be easily crossed. Some
accepted this as part of the unusual gifts that made him the poet he was;
others found it disconcerting. This pride is easy to understand in a different
age, but at that time people were expected to know their place, and Burns
upset the standard arrangements not by crass defiance, but by some subtle
quality that caught people off balance. A generation later Thomas Carlyle
found himself entering a not dissimilar situation, and perhaps that helped
him to what was an acute insight: 'The peasant poet bears himself ... like a
king in exile: he is cast among the low and feels himself equal to the highest,
yet he claims no rank, that none may be disputed to him'. Part of Burns's
love for Glencairn was that the Earl behaved just as Burns himself would
have, had their situations been reversed.

Glencairn was also a Freemason. For Burns, this fraternity concentrated
political values and personal experience. It provided the network of personal contact that opened doors throughout the poet's life as effectively as
the patronage of Glencairn. Stewart Watson's nineteenth-century painting
of Burns's reception as 'poet laureate' at Lodge Canongate Kilwinning in
Edinburgh shows a spectacular event which did not happen: Burns *was*
inducted and a handsome toast proposed to him, but the picture includes

94

enthusiastic masons who were not there, such as James Boswell. It is a theoretical muster of some of the most influential people of the time. It is sometimes supposed that Freemasonry thus gave Burns a convenient leg up among people of influence just when he needed it. It ran much deeper than that.

Burns's brand of patriotism and egalitarianism could be accommodated and even encouraged in the world that he found at the outset of his public fame. His ideas were still forming and had not been crystallised by events, but the world of Freemasonry also helped that process. This movement probably had its origin in the old craftsmen's incorporations. The earliest known individual organiser was William Schaw, Master of Works to James VI in the late sixteenth century. He signed himself General Warden of the Masons of Scotland and produced two books of statutes to govern the organisation. During the seventeenth century such an organisation was changing, the first non-operative 'masons' – that is, those not practising the skills of the trade – appearing in the 1630s. By the end of the century some lodges were dominated by gentlemen, but they continued the 'Mason Word' of personal identification and ritual. In 1710 there were some twenty-five lodges throughout the Lowlands.

In the eighteenth century, the movement became identified with ideas of brotherhood that overstepped the boundaries of rank and nation. Its international influence grew after its fashionable adoption in England and the foundation of a grand lodge in that country in 1717. Throughout Europe, Freemasonry became identified with the constitutional values of the 'Glorious Revolution' of 1688–9 in England and Scotland. For that reason Freemasons were persecuted in France in the 1740s, as they were identified as a British export; they were an organisation in a country that then tolerated no organisations other than church and state. Later a German masonic almanac of 1776 spoke of how 'nations are enlightened ... unified through humane and social politics'.

Freemasonry also developed a mythos of ancient origins that far antedated the coming of Christ, and was connected with the building of the Pyramids and the Temple of Solomon. This was not an appeal to antiquity for its own sake. In a movement where symbols were fundamental means of expression, such examples of well-conceived architecture reflected a vision of society in which every member had a necessary place as part of the structure. Such symbols from a remote past also had one outstanding advantage: they were not emotionally charged. In particular, they were not entangled with religion. In the eighteenth century this was not an easy thing to do. Even today, the mention of the National Covenant of 1638 or the Solemn League and Covenant of 1643 can stir anyone familiar with

Procession of St
James's Lodge,
Tarbolton, etched
after a painting by D.
O. Hill. In the
eighteenth century,
Freemasons had a
public as well as
private face. Burns
was Depute Master of
St James's for four
years from 1784.
From *The Land of
Burns*.

NATIONAL LIBRARY OF
SCOTLAND

Scottish history – either for or against. For Burns the Covenanting times were still a living memory, as his mother had been partly brought up by her grandmother, whose memory went back to the times of the religious wars.

The Covenants were one expression of a common currency among orthodox Calvinists throughout Europe and those who had gone to the American colonies to escape persecution: the notion of religious and civil life not just governed but guaranteed by contract. As we have seen, orthodox Calvinism soon revised the early reformers' understanding of the relationship between God and humanity, making it legalistic and conditional. This legalism was also applied on a social scale, the Scriptures being ransacked for evidence of contractual relationships between God and whole peoples. This was not an arbitrary God, but one who had figured out a legal framework, as in the Ten Commandments, where an eye for an eye was a merciful exercise in moderation. When applied to a queen or king and their subjects, mutual obligation meant that neither people nor sovereign were above the law, and those who stuck their heads above that framework were liable to have them parted from their necks. When John Milton wrote his *Defence of the People of England* after the beheading of Charles I in 1649, he relied heavily on George Buchanan's *De Iure Regni Apud Scotos*

96

(the rights of the Crown concerning the Scots) which he had written in 1569 to justify the way that Mary, Queen of Scots, had been forced to abdicate two years earlier. It was part of the politico-religious attitude that would lead to notions of a 'social contract' between rulers and ruled. Freemasonry converted ideas that were once the currency of vicious civil strife into liberal politics by extracting the constitutional element and quite deliberately setting it against religious zealotry. Thus Freemasonry adhered to a generally beneficent deism rather than a closely defined creed, and this on occasion brought it into collision with organised religion.

The aims of Freemasonry thus meant much more than people being nice to one another. On the eve of the French Revolution the Grand Lodge of Scotland might be corresponding with numerous lodges in France on the basis of *La Douce Harmonie* and *Ardente Humanité*, but that was a coded language for much more, and is related to another characteristic, which was the way the movement ran itself. Freemasonry was meant to be the pattern for a good state. The ancient Greek legislators Lycurgus and Solon were masonic heroes as models of wisdom and law-giving. Masonic rhetoric gloried in republics, and that was reflected in the quasi-republican order in which even the highest offices were subject to election. And as in the republics of old, the citizenship did not include the rabble, but those whose education qualified them to participate. The membership of the eighteenth-century lodges probably corresponded to the limited franchise effected by the Reform Act of 1832. So when Burns was initiated into St David's Lodge in Tarbolton in 1781, Freemasonry was identified with liberal politics and thought. In Germany and France adherents saw it as a happy British export, reflecting the best values of the 'Glorious Revolution' of 1688–9 which they wanted for themselves.

Then came a real republic bred of the American Revolution. There Benjamin Franklin had been a particularly active mason. Nine signatories of the Declaration of Independence and thirteen of the Constitution of the United States were Freemasons. When George Washington laid the foundation stone of the Executive Mansion, the forerunner of the White House, he did so in full masonic regalia. To this day, a United States one dollar bill carries symbols of Freemasonry.

The attempt to crush the American colonists was initially popular in Scotland, because of the severe damage to the vested interests in the tobacco trade, but that passed as the war went from bad to worse. It was just possible to be pro-colonist and not be charged with sedition. The 'Ballad on the American War' lampoons the war without drawing any fundamental conclusions about the British constitution. The war had blown over enough

Thomas Paine (1737–1809), author of *The Rights of Man* and *bête noire* of the political establishment in Britain in the late eighteenth century. A copy based on a portrait by George Romney.

for it to be included in the Edinburgh edition.

However, with the 'Address of Beelzebub' we are moving into different and turbulent waters. The Highland Society had been established two years before in 1784 by leading landowners and agriculturalists as a kind of development agency. Although it was part of the mainstream of farming improvement, it also reflected the shock of the loss of the American colonies, and the consequent mood of retrenchment. The Highlands had proved a source of excellent soldiers during both the Seven Years War and the American War, and the government was reluctant to lose this. Also, there was still a crude belief that a country's strength lay in its manpower. On a practical level, block emigration from an area was financially embarrassing to the laird, because his rents were gone at a stroke.

So when five hundred Highlanders prepared to emigrate from the lands of MacDonnell of Glengarry, the Highland Society met to consider means of frustrating them. This was reported in the *Edinburgh Advertiser*, and aroused Burns's wrath. Glengarry in particular was a vicious and unruly character, bordering on the insane. At the turn of the century he would not be trying to retain his people but be evicting them wholesale. What enraged Burns was the treating of people like property. As the Devil advises Glengarry:

> *But smash them! crush them a' to spails,*
> *An' rot the dyvors i' the jails!*
> *The young dogs swinge them to the labour:*
> *Let wark an hunger mak them sober!*

And here also are John Hancock, who was the first to sign the Declaration of Independence; Benjamin Franklin, who had a considerable part in writing the Constitution; George Washington, who had defeated the British government forces; and Richard Montgomery, a British professional soldier who had gone over to the colonists' side and perished in their cause. With such leadership:

> *…(God knows what may be effected*
> *When by such heads and hearts directed)*
> *Poor dunghill sons of dirt an mire*
> *May to Patrician rights aspire!*

Beneath the deft wit there now lies real and dangerous anger. As Thomas Paine remarked in his *Common Sense* (1776), the pamphlet that did much to stiffen the colonists' resolve in their worst hour, 'by referring the matter from argument to arms, a new era for politics is struck, a new method of thinking hath arisen'.

There are two kinds of rebels: those that understand authority, and those that do not. Burns was among the first; Thomas Muir of Huntershill was among the latter, and was doomed to martyrdom. Muir was an advocate who had taken the part of the common people. He was charged with sedition in January 1793, released on bail and brought to trial at the end of August. Popular myth has it that in his concluding speech for his own defence, Muir pled that even Christ himself was a reformer. 'And mukkil guid that did him', Lord Braxfield, the presiding judge, is said to have commented: 'He wes hingit, m'n, he wes hingit'. Braxfield did in fact articulate the law as it stood. 'In this country [the government] is made up of the landed interest, which alone has a right to be represented; as for the rabble, who have nothing but personal property, what hold has the nation of them?' Muir was an advocate and defended himself. As the saying has it, the lawyer who pleads in his own cause has a fool for a client. In his moving speech, Muir supplied the prosecution with what it needed: proof of intention to break the laws of sedition. He got fourteen years' transportation.

Thomas Muir of Huntershill (1765–98), chalk drawing by David Martin. A handsome monument to this advocate and martyr in the Radical cause still stands in the Calton burial ground in Edinburgh.

Muir was also found guilty of distributing Thomas Paine's *The Rights of Man* (1791–2), which had been banned the previous year. It spelt out numerous home truths in simple yet eloquent English, with the occasional wisecrack that probably had Burns himself roaring with laughter. It included a thrilling description of the events leading to the storming of the Bastille, from which John Reed could have got his pattern for *Ten Days That Shook the World* (1926), the classic eye–witness account in English of the point when the Bolshevik Revolution swung in the balance. The main burden of Paine's message was the absurdity of the vast incubus of inherited rights of the French and British ruling establishments. There is little that Burns would have disagreed with. 'The circumstances of the world are continually changing, and so the opinions of men change also; and as government is for the living, and not for the dead, it is the living only that has any right in it'. What would have gone straight to Burns's heart were Paine's opening remarks, in which he pointed to the madness of Britain and France continually worrying each other:

Robert Macqueen,
Lord Braxfield
(1722–98), by Sir
Henry Raeburn,
c. 1798. Lord Justice
Clerk Braxfield
figured in Burns's life
a decade before the
trial of Thomas Muir.
As the Lord
Ordinary, he gave
final judgement in
the litigation over
rent between Burns's
father William and
his landlord, the Ayr
merchant David
McLure of
Shawwood.

*I had seen enough of the miseries of war, to wish it
might never more have existence in the world, and
that some other mode might be found out to settle
the differences that should occasionally arise in the
neighbourhood of nations ...*

And he reminded readers:

*That there are men in all countries who get their
living by war, and by keeping up the quarrels of
Nations, is as shocking as it is true.*

Paine suggested that if national policy were put
in the hands of the people who had to suffer the consequences, and there were rational communication
between such governments, war would stop. This re-
flected the idealistic element Burns had found in Freemasonry. At the start
of the French Revolution, many in Britain had applauded, supposing that
the French were merely emulating the British settlement of 1688–9. Edmund
Burke's *Reflections on the Revolution in France* (1790) helped reverse this
into a mood of black reaction in government and the respectable classes,
while popular enthusiasm marched on.

One thing Paine shared with Burns was that he was a former exciseman.
The government was totally dependent on the efficient conduct of the Excise
to raise the taxes by which it financed its activities. Yet the excisemen were
traditionally a troublesome lot, especially in Scotland. During the '45 some
of them had carried on raising revenue, but for Prince Charles Edward
Stuart. When hints of Burns's enthusiasm for the French Revolution reached
the ears of the authorities in Edinburgh, he was in trouble. Immediately
Burns bolted for cover, for on 5 January 1793 he wrote a pleading letter to
Graham of Fintry, the man who had secured him his post:

*As to REFORM PRINCIPLES, I look upon the British Constitution,
as settled at the Revolution, to be the most glorious Constitution on
earth, or that perhaps the wit of man can frame; at the same time, I
think, & you know what High and distinguished Characters have for
some time thought so, that we have a good deal deviated from the original
principles of that Constitution ... As to France, I was her enthusiastic
votary in the beginning of the business. – When she came to shew her old
avidity for conquest, in annexing Savoy, &c. to her dominions, &*

invading the rights of Holland, I altered my sentiments.

It was a very astute reply, because there was still enough reforming politics in it to sound convincing (and seriously irritate Fintry's fellow commissioners) but not enough to demand drastic action. There was a gentlemanly investigation and the matter fizzled out. As long as Burns bridled his tongue he was safe. He had also got in his word just in time. Sixteen days later King Louis XVI of France was executed (despite the pleas of Paine and Muir among others), and on 1 February 1793 France declared war on Britain.

Probably the most important element in Burns's 'acquittal' was his disavowal of involvement in any organisation or clandestine activity, because that was what authority feared, and not without reason. The *raibble* was not the uneducated *canaille*, which in Braxfield's view had no political rights, it was the urban mob. This unstable monster could champion a Catholic pogrom, as in the Gordon riots in London in 1779, as readily as the weavers' riots for a living wage in Glasgow in 1785. Burns had the countryman's aversion to violent tumult. When there was a hissing of 'God Save the King' and a call for revolutionary songs at the Dumfries playhouse, he considered it beneath him 'to yell in the howlings of a rabble'. He chose the path he knew – the pen.

The outcome of Thomas Muir's trial shocked Burns, as indeed it was meant to shock all radically minded people. His response was to send George Thomson 'Scots wha hae wi Wallace bled':

> *Wha for Scotland's King and Law*
> *Freedom's sword will strongly draw,*
> *Freeman stand, or Freeman fa',*
> *Let him follow me!*

Six months later he sent it to the London *Morning Chronicle*. The reference to 'Liberty' and 'Tyrants' in the poem was language that would then be plainly understood as incendiary, and Burns asked that it be published 'as a thing they have met with by accident'. Three months on he composed his 'Ode for General Washington's Birthday'. This time written in Augustan English, the passion still bursts through the grand phrase. He speaks of the fledgling United States:

General Charles
François du Périer
Dumouriez (1739–
1823) by Jean
Sébastien Rouillard.
Burns was disgusted
when Dumouriez
deserted the
revolutionary cause –
before the Terror and
its busy guillotine.
MUSÉE NATIONAL DU CHÂTEAU
DE VERSAILLES

In danger's hour still flaming in the van,
Ye know, and dare maintain the Royalty of Man!

Although Burns was careful to watch what he
said in public, his views and those of his friends
William Maxwell and John Syme were well enough
known in Dumfries. The Dumfries Loyal Natives
were a group of strenuous conservatives formed in
January 1773, and Burns was named in their lampoons. It was they who now courted 'the rabble', and
he despised them for it. When shown some of their
productions, on the spur of the moment he replied:

Ye true 'Loyal Natives' attend to my song:
In uproar and riot rejoice the night long!
From Envy and Hatred your core is exempt,
But where is your shield from the darts of
Contempt?

Yet the fact was that those holding radical views were being steadily
pushed into an embattled minority, not by the Loyalists or their rabble, but
by events.

In his *apologia* to Graham of Fintry Burns also enclosed a copy of his ribald
'Why shouldna poor folk mowe', in which the monarchs of Europe are
urged to indulge the joys of the flesh in the same spirit as their poor subjects. He mentions the Prussian reverse at Valmy, where the Duke of Brunswick was forced to retreat instead of continuing his progress to Paris to
reinstate the old order. He also notes the second partition of Poland:

Auld Kate laid her claws on poor Stanislaus,
And Poland has bent like a bow

For the author of 'Scots Wha Hae' the destruction of Poland must
have seemed a miserable business. What would not have been obvious at
the time was that the Duke of Brunswick's invasion of France was a half-
hearted side-show. Prussia, Russia and Austria were more consumed with
their greed for a slice of Poland than crushing the new Republic. A new
French army was raked together from the wreck of the old and from volunteers. Over the coming years it would grow without interruption, swelled

by conscription. As the Jacobins took control of government, the minds of its commanders were concentrated by the consequence of failure – execution. Dumouriez, the victor of Valmy, Jemappes and Neerwinden thought it prudent to desert the Republic, provoking Burns's contempt:

> *Then let us fight about*
> *Till Freedom's spark be out,*
> *Then we'll be damn'd, no doubt, Dumourier.*
>
> ON GENERAL DUMOURIER'S DESERTION

What Burns could not know was that Dumouriez was in favour of a moderate constitutional monarchy, and that the army had refused to back him. Instead the cry was for 'a war of the Peoples against the Kings'. Revolution was becoming entwined with resurgent French nationalism, the same mixture that would inspire 'Scots Wha Hae'. Robespierre was against a foreign crusade, fearing the consequences, but he was shouted down. The crisis that followed brought him to power, and also, as an emergency wartime measure, the Committee for Public Safety.

As events unfolded into 1793, that dawn of July 1789 must have seemed a mighty distance away to Tom Paine. 'Whom has the National Assembly brought to the scaffold? None,' he had written. Even his heroes, such as the Marquis de Lafayette, had now fled the storm, and he found

The Execution of Marie Antoinette, engraved by Helman from a painting by Charles Monnet. After the French monarchy was abolished by decree in September 1792, Louis XVI was guillotined the following January, and his queen-consort on 16 October 1793. Her fate was sealed by revelations of her plans for a bloody counter-revolution.

BIBLIOTHÈQUE NATIONALE, PARIS

himself in a Paris jail awaiting the fall of the knife. He was only saved when the terrible Robespierre himself was cornered by his terrified fellow Convention members and guillotined with ninety-two other Jacobins at the end of July 1794. Apart from the two thousand and six hundred who had been formally executed in Paris, countless others had perished throughout France, whether in indiscriminate murder or the butchery that followed the crushing of counter-revolution. The jails of France were crammed with over a quarter of a million 'suspects'. Following the fall of Robespierre there came the 'White Terror' of reaction and revenge.

All this was widely reported in the British press. Nevertheless, shortly after that Burns wrote to Mrs Dunlop on 12 January 1795 with his now famous comments about 'the deserved fate of a certain pair of Personages [the execution of King Louis and Queen Marie-Antoinette of France], – What is there in the delivering over a perjured Blockhead & an unprincipled Prostitute into the hands of the hangman...'. This:

> *When the welfare of millions is hung in the scale,*
> *And the balance yet trembles with fate?*

Burns was quoting from William Roscoe's 'O'er the vine-covered hills and gay regions of France?'.

Burns's contempt for hereditary privilege was unconquerable, even when he should have thought about whom he was addressing. One of Mrs Dunlop's sons was an officer in the British army, then at war with the French. Two of her daughters were married to Frenchmen who had fled the Revolution. Little wonder that she was *black affrontit*. She ignored Burns until he was dying, when she relented. Yet, interestingly, she appears to have kept the details to herself, for when the poet ran into her son a year later, he did not appear to hint at what had offended his mother. Even in this silence there was a loyalty which overruled severe provocation. And despite the lack of tact, Burns was motivated by more than some blind prejudice. Far from accepting the constitutional monarchy that was on offer, Queen Marie-Antoinette in particular had been plotting to bring back absolute monarchy, and before she and her husband had been threatened with execution her brother-in-law Charles was stomping Europe with a band of reactionary emigrés at his back describing in fearsome terms what he would do to the revolutionaries. All this was made public at the time, and Burns would have been incensed by it.

It is unlikely that we will ever know if Burns wrote 'The Tree of Liberty', as apparently no manuscript has survived. It contains lines which if they are not Burns's, are certainly a reflection of his thought:

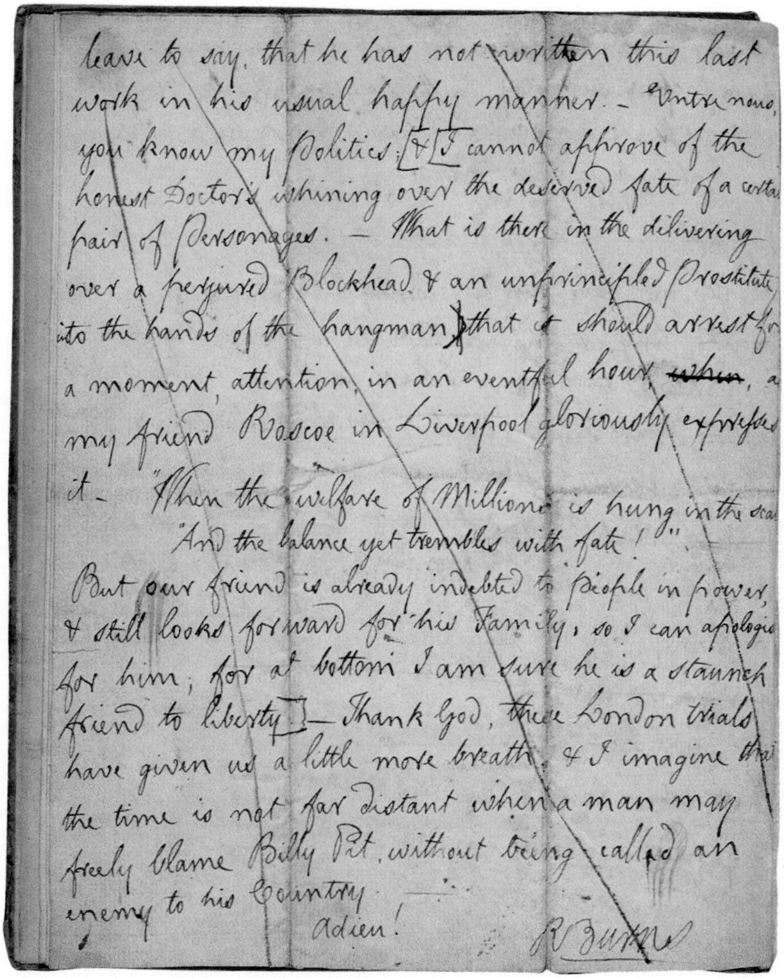

Upo' this tree there grows sic fruit,
Its virtues a' can tell, man;
It raises man aboon the brute,
It maks him ken himsel, man.

Tom Paine's vision is put neatly in four lines:

Wi plenty o sic trees, I trow,
The warld would live in peace, man;
The sword would help to mak a plough,
The din o war wad cease, man.

105

The REPUBLICAN-ATTACK.

The Republican Attack, by James Gillray. It depicts the point at which government fears of the French Revolution crossing the English Channel came to a head. On 29 October 1795 the window of King George III's coach was shattered by a projectile thrown by the London mob. In the cartoon, William Pitt (the driver) and Henry Dundas (in a plaid) disdain the leaders of the opposition, who are portrayed as a gang of vicious *sans-culottes*.

BRITISH MUSEUM

Rather, the din would get worse. What was becoming a 'Republic of Proprietors' had an effective army of over eight hundred thousand men, the first mass army in modern Europe. For those who had been party to regicide, for the war profiteers and for the newly empowered *bourgeoisie*, there was no going back, except perhaps to avenge the humiliations inflicted by Britain on France during the Seven Years War four decades before. The Republic had succeeded where the greatest generals of the Bourbons had failed, for France had swallowed up Belgium, now reached to the Rhine down nearly all of its west bank, controlled the Netherlands, and had also made other acquisitions such as Nice and Savoy. By the end of 1794 all the Continental powers had made their peace with France. William Pitt, who himself loathed the idea of war, now warned Britain to prepare for a French invasion.

On 31 January 1795 Burns became one of the founder members of the Royal Dumfries Volunteers. But he was not signing up to someone else's outfit for the sake of form. The way in which the Volunteers was run showed an underlying change of attitude that was already taking place in

British politics, and in fact the government heartily disliked it. The officers were elected by the Volunteers, and the organisation was run by a committee, of which Burns was an active member. The government would chip away at the Volunteers' character until by 1808 they had effectively bridled what independence they had, and had roped them into the local militia, which was under direct government control.

About this time Burns wrote two songs. One was 'A Man's a Man for a' that'.

> *It's comin yet for a' that,*
> *That man to man, the world, o'er*
> *Shall brithers be for a' that.*

In the circumstances, that was optimism indeed – either that or a defiant idealism in the face of events. The other song was more apposite to the moment:

> *Does haughty Gaul invasion threat?*
> *Then let the loons beware, Sir!*
> *There's wooden walls upon our seas*
> *And volunteers on shore, Sir!*

Indeed, the song contained squibs of defiant ambiguity:

> *For never but by British hands*
> *Maun British wrangs be righted!*
> DOES HAUGHTY GAUL INVASION THREAT?

It was vastly popular at the time, but who has ever heard it sung now? In the end Burns's vision, but not his optimism, has been vindicated. In the twentieth century, which has seen mass brutality and murder transformed into an industry, 'A Man's a Man' has been the internationale of human decency and common sense. It is sung by ordinary women and men long after *The Rights of Man* is largely forgotten. But Tom Paine must have loved it.

CHAPTER SIX

CALEDONIA'S BARD

On 27 November 1786 Robert Burns mounted a borrowed *pownie* and headed east to Scotland's capital. He was no stranger to towns, for he was familiar with Ayr, Irvine and Kilmarnock, all of them ancient burghs, and the first the centre of the county's administration. Yet Edinburgh was different. Despite Glasgow's growing size and prosperity, with a population of over seventy thousand, Edinburgh was still bigger. It was the metropolis of Scotland. Far from declining with the Union of the Parliaments, the capital was prospering. About eighteen years before Burns came to Edinburgh the decision had been taken to expand the city into the New Town, but even before this significant development was under way, housing overflowed from the Cowgate into the Southside.

William Burnes had had a part in the city's expansion. The Borough or South Loch was part of the city's defences that had foiled Cromwell in the middle of the previous century. After the failure of the Jacobite cause in 1746, that barrier was no longer necessary. After it had been drained, William was one of the landscape gardeners laying out the new Meadows. Thus Robert would have had at least some idea of Edinburgh from his father.

He was, after a fashion, going there to seek his fortune, and, also after a fashion, he found it. The proceeds of his Edinburgh edition of his poems – about eight hundred pounds – were a considerable sum in those days, and the personal contacts he made would lead to others that secured him a place in the Excise Service, and with it financial security. What he also found was fame, and that fame would expose what were very personal attitudes to public scrutiny, both in his own day and after. Far from some systematic philosophical manifesto, we are often confronted with paradox. Things are not always what they seem, nor do the poet's words and actions fall into the coherent patterns so convenient to hindsight.

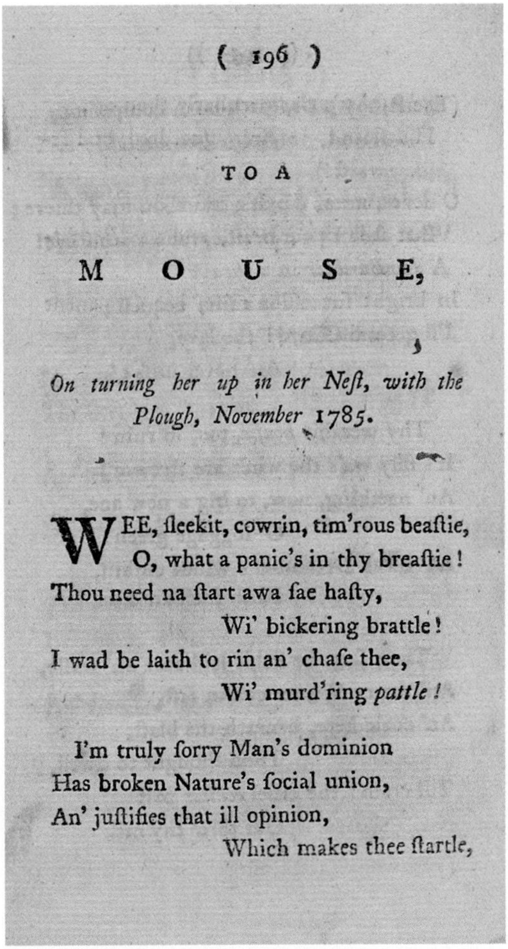

(196)

T O A

M O U S E,

On turning her up in her Neft, with the
Plough, November 1785.

WEE, fleekit, cowrin, tim'rous beaftie,
   O, what a panic's in thy breaftie !
Thou need na ftart awa fae hafty,
         Wi' bickering brattle !
I wad be laith to rin an' chafe thee,
         Wi' murd'ring *pattle* !

I'm truly forry Man's dominion
Has broken Nature's focial union,
An' juftifies that ill opinion,
         Which makes thee ftartle,

The opening stanzas
of 'To A Mouse',
from the first
Edinburgh edition of
Burns's poems,
published on 21 April
1787.

   This journey to Edinburgh was Burns's first beyond his native heath. It took him along and up the river Ayr and out on to the moors, where many of the surrounding hills rise to over fifteen hundred feet. He would have passed the lonely Covenanters' graves at Glenbuck, and at Muirkirk he would have noticed the first transformation from the lonely moorland village with its one inn. Construction work had started on the new iron works, and the tar works that John McAdam of road-making fame would manage. Over the watershed and down the Douglas Water lay Hyndford Brig and the Clyde. Then he made a small but significant diversion, to Covington Mains, where on the signal of his arrival farmers came in from the surrounding countryside to meet the poet. The gathering continued early into the following morning.

The West Bow from the Lawnmarket by Thomas H. Shepherd. Burns's first Edinburgh lodging was in the nearby Baxter's Close, on the north side of the High Street (the site of the present Lady Stair's Close).

EDINBURGH CITY COUNCIL, LIBRARIES & MUSEUMS

That gathering at Covington Mains might seem a pleasant minor incident that preceded Burns's triumphal reception in the capital, but it was ultimately more significant. The farmers of a remote upland district had congregated to honour not just a fellow farmer, but a poet. In the following centuries statues would appear throughout Europe of fearsome warrior saints and heroes from a distant past: St George slaying his dragon and Boadicea on her scythed chariot at Westminster, a noble Wenceslas in the Václavské námestí (Wenceslas Square) in Prague and a truly terrible St Michael presiding over his glorious dead at the monument to the 1814 Battle of the Nations at Leipzig. Scotland has her share, the helmed and mailed figures of Wallace and Bruce, striding and riding to fields of death or glory. It is the measure of Burns's achievement that he has more than rivalled these grim and shadowy house-gods in his position as a national hero. Those farmers of upper Clydesdale were the first to recognise Burns in such a deliberate way.

Eighteenth-century Scotland was not just some economic backwater that was being transformed by trade. Just before the turn of the seventeenth century John Slezer had published his *Theatrum Scotiae*. In the finely en-

graved views of the principal Burghs, the magnificent ruins of a glorious past figured large, as well
as cathedrals and palaces that would not have been
out of place in other more opulent countries. Burns
and others were also conscious of an ancient and
independent history, their sights on the glories of
what even in the eighteenth century was a distant
past: the Wars of Independence. These old battles
had been centred on a struggle in the first instance
with Edward I of England. In his day Edward had
been the paragon of European chivalry, but in old
age his character had degenerated. Territorial greed
got the better of him, and when this was thwarted,
he reacted with a terrifying viciousness. When his
schemes to be recognised as the overlord of Scotland first came unstuck in 1296 he laid waste to
the town of Berwick. Then part of Scotland, and

by far the biggest settlement, the town was not only put to the torch, but
the inhabitants were massacred. It was one of those atrocities that ranks
with the sack of Magdeburg in the Thirty Years War, or of Drogheda by
Cromwell. The result was two-fold: first, there were centuries of fruitless
enmity and mistrust between Scotland and England and second, an
untouchably heroic status for the two people who, against apparently hopeless odds, rid the land of the tyrant's yoke – Sir William Wallace and King
Robert, the Bruce.

Patrick Miller of
Dalswinton (1731–
1815) by Sir George
Chalmers. Reforming
landowner, inventor
and entrepreneur,
Patrick Miller was
one of a clutch of
individuals
prominent in the
agricultural and
industrial revolutions
of the eighteenth
century who were
quick to recognise
Burns's merits, and
offer him their
patronage. But
Burns's talents and
energies failed to
secure him rewards to
match – a fact which
Thomas Carlyle later
put down to a 'want
of unity in his
purposes, of
consistency in his
aims'.

NATIONAL PORTRAIT GALLERY,
LONDON

In practical terms, when the old papist Kirk was overthrown in
Scotland in 1560, Scotland and England now found themselves in the same
political and religious camp for the first time. Here was the start of laying
the old enmities to rest. When James VI succeeded to the English throne in
1603, had there also been a union of Parliaments at the same time, the
whole sense of Scotland's identity would have been different and probably
much less remarkable. As it was, the union of the Scottish and English
Parliaments would take place in 1707, and a new British state would be
created. Yet paradoxically it was the century in between, the seventeenth
century, that created the Scotland that was really different. This difference
might be coloured by ethnicity, but at the heart of it lay ideas. Religious
and constitutional thought, the universities and education, and not least
the law, all developed a substance of some considerable intellectual weight.

This is not surprising. Besides the advance of revolutionary thought
that we have considered, in the circumstances of 1603 pressure towards

Robert Burns's
Tours of the
Highlands,
Stirlingshire
& the Borders

0   10   20   40   60
MILES

INVERNESS   CULLODEN   ELGIN
FALLS
OF
FOYERS   AVIEMORE   PETERHEAD
KINGUSSIE
ABERDEEN
STONEHAVEN
BRAWLIE MUIR
MONTROSE
KENMORE   DUNKELD
PERTH   ARBROATH
INVERARAY   DUNDEE
TARBET
DUNBLANE   North Sea
STIRLING
TARBERT   BANNOCKBURN
DUMBARTON   DUNFERMLINE
FALKIRK
PAISLEY   GLASGOW   LINLITHGOW
DUNBAR
EDINBURGH
EYEMOUTH
DUNS
MAUCHLINE
TRAQUAIR   COLDSTREAM
MELROSE   KELSO   BERWICK
SELKIRK   JEDBURGH
– – TOUR of the BORDERS
– – TOUR of WEST HIGHLANDS   DUMFRIES   WAUCHOPE   WARKWORTH
ANNAN
– – TOUR of HIGHLANDS
MORPETH
– – TOUR of STIRLINGSHIRE
CARLISLE   Hadrian's Wall
HEXHAM   NEWCASTLE

Burns's tours around
Scotland.

legislative union was obvious. The king and others suggested it, and there were various points at which union was effected during the century both in church and state, only to drift apart again. The natural instinct was to develop national and institutional assets that could be placed on the negotiating table. The Union of the Parliaments in 1707 traded away the legislature against leaving the religious and legal framework largely intact.

The Scottish Parliament was different in character from, and less developed than, the English one. Until near the end of its existence, it had been much more under the direct control of the Crown. The commissioners were delegates rather than members, charged with bringing home concessions and opportunities for those who had elected them. How much greater would the opportunities for that be in London! To those who would benefit directly, the Union was common sense. To those who would not benefit, the Unionists were in Burns's words 'a parcel of rogues'.

If there was a constitutional soul of the nation, it lay in the Kirk and the law. In the Kirk that soul was a form of orthodox Calvinism, one that thought in terms of two kingdoms: this kingdom of Caesar's and Christ's kingdom in eternity. Nor was the legal constitution of Caesar's kingdom neglected. Legal writers such as the Earl of Stair and Mackenzie of Rosehaugh understood civil law as the cement of a 'weil governit commonweil'. It created the framework for everyday comings and goings, from rights of property and conditions of trade to marriage and inheritance. In a society where economic change was slow, people did not then foresee a demand for legal change in the future, and in the medium term they were right. The Kirk and legal establishment would have various tussles with the new English-dominated Parliament, but as we will see, the old framework and climate very much remained until the reform of the Union Parliament in 1832–3. This created a new animal with a legislative appetite that would overrule and erode the old structures.

Of course, the one part of Scotland that appears to be left out of this equation is that considerable third that lay beyond the Highland line, speaking a different language and with a formidable literary and musical tradition of its own. But events would not let the Highlands alone any more than the Lowlands. If the eighteenth century brought England and Lowland Scotland closer, it would also see Scotland herself become two nations.

This was of intense interest to Burns. Much of his patriotism and sense of nation derived unconsciously from that storehouse of ideas generated in the previous century. The latter-day *narodnik* back-to-the-land chauvinist with his knuckles trailing among blood and soil would have horrified Burns. He expressed himself in Scots language and song because that was the poetic face of his *Heimat*. The *Auld Scotia* of which he spoke with such affection and which he ventured to travel with such curiosity included the Gaelic-speaking Highlands as much as the Scots-speaking Lowlands. His concept of the Scotland he loved and fought for was free of ethnic incubus. At its heart was a different and infinitely more enduring substance – liberty, and recognition of the dignity that could exist in even the poorest of people. He wanted these values not just as state condescension to freedom of conscience, or an uncertain reward from an unseen divinity, but for them to be tangible, in the ethos of the community of which he was a part. For there was also that old Scotland which Burns loathed and with which he battled – intellectual curiosity and passion corrupted to arrogance and intolerance,

My Heart's in the
Highlands, by
Horatio McCulloch,
1860.

*My heart's in the
Highlands, my heart
is not here
My heart's in the
Highlands,
a-chasing the deer.*

As living memory of
the Jacobite rising of
1745 faded, Burns's
interest in the
Highlands would be
commandeered to
reinforce the
romantic image of the
land of the mountain
and the flood, his
blistering 'Address of
Beelzebub'
conveniently
overlooked.

and the pride of a community's history commandeered for pride of family
as if it were a personal possession.

The Jacobite risings of 1715 and 1745 and the French Revolution of 1789
may seem so far removed from one another as to have little connection.
The risings were brief flames of insurrection in a remote and little-known
region of north west Europe. They caused only a moment's tremor to the
established order of a growing mercantile empire. The French Revolution
overturned a splendid monarchy and reorganised the state. Yet the links
between the two events are worth noting. They are paralleled by two other
events also involving Scotland and France, and which quite disturbed late
sixteenth-century Europe. The first was the deposition of Mary, Queen of
Scots, in 1567 by her subjects (and also her subsequent execution by Elizabeth I of England). The second was the slaughter of the French protestants
on the eve of the feast of St Bartholomew in 1572. What were the rights of
a sovereign? Could her subjects simply dispose of her right to be queen?
And what were the rights of a subject? Could a king dispose of those he did
not like, or connive at their destruction, and if not, why not?

Both the Jacobite risings and the French Revolution reflected the same ideological core, but reversed the polarity of the countries involved. The risings looked to the traditional values of patriarchal kingship. Since all major European states at the time were monarchies (bar the Dutch Republic, with which Lowland Scotland had very close ties), the philosophy of kingship was a legitimate concern. That 'there's such divinity doth hedge a king' was very real. This is expressed in one of the greatest pibrochs, probably composed by Padruig Mór MacCrimmon at Stirling, on the march to the ill-fated battle of Worcester in 1651, 'Fhuair mi pòg o làimh an Righ' (I got a kiss of the King's hand). In practical terms the Stuart kings did little enough for the *Gaidhealtachd*, and indeed much to destroy it, yet in 1745 it was the idea of kingship as much as personal loyalty that could draw the noble Locheil on to a path that he knew would lead to certain ruin. On the other hand the French Revolution was an expression of aggressive rationality. Once that included the trial and execution of the king, then the Revolution had shot to the opposite pole from Jacobitism. Yet there was one significant factor common to both events: they started with constitutional aims but they ended as vehicles of nationalism. Burns had a sense of personal connection with both events. He supposed that his father's father might have been 'out' in the '15, and he lived to see the French Revolution degenerate into chauvinist cruelty.

There is no evidence one way or another that the Burnes family followed the Jacobite Earl Marischal in the '15. Yet in a letter of 16 December 1789 to Lady Winifred Maxwell Constable, the daughter of the Jacobite Earl of Nithsdale, Burns identifies strongly with the Jacobite cause:

> *What they could they did, and what they had they lost: with unshaken firmness and unconcealed Political Attachments, they shook hands with Ruin for what they esteemed the cause of their King and their Country.*

Burns's Edinburgh schoolmaster friend William Nicol and various others he knew were nominal 'Jacobites'. Burns attended Jacobite dinners in the full knowledge that the cause itself was utterly dead. In striking Augustan English, on 31 December 1787, he marked the birthday of the now elderly and decrepit but one time 'Bonnie Prince Charlie' with a 'Birthday Ode':

> *False flatterer, Hope, away,*
> *Nor think to lure us as in days of yore!*
> *We solemnize this sorrowing natal day,*
> *To prove our loyal truth—we can no more*

Jane Gordon, Duchess of Gordon (1746–1812), with her son the Marquess of Huntly (later 5th Duke of Gordon). She was one of the presiding society beauties and characters that Burns encountered when he came to Edinburgh in 1786. Painted by George Romney in 1778.

SCOTTISH NATIONAL PORTRAIT GALLERY

That was a conclusion that Prince Charles Edward himself had reached many years before. One month after the birthday ode, the Prince died. That left his younger brother Henry, who had risen to be the Bishop of Frascati and a cardinal. Henry had a comfortable income from the revenues of two French abbeys, but the Revolution put a stop to that. The benevolent George III gave him a pension of four thousand pounds a year. His grandfather James VII had taken the English crown jewels with him into exile and Henry still had them. When he died in 1807 Henry left them to George, Prince of Wales. Against that background, flourishes of Jacobite sentiment were either sentimentality, or a front for something else.

The same year as Prince Charles Edward's death was the centenary of the overthrow of his grandfather in the 'Glorious Revolution' of 1688. The tenor of the celebrations, particularly the pronouncements from various pulpits, provoked Burns to write a letter to the *Edinburgh Evening Courant* published on 22 November under the pseudonym of 'A Briton'. He was disturbed at 'the harsh abusive manner' in which the Stuarts were denounced, with no allowance being made for the different age and circumstances in which they lived. 'At that period, the science of government—the true relation between King and subject, like other sciences, was but in its infancy, emerging from the dark ages of ignorance and barbarism'. William and Mary 'owed the throne solely to the call of a free people'. Burns expressed relief that the Stuarts had failed in the attempts of 1715 and 1745, but could not join others in condemning and laughing at their folly or impracticality. He then held up the example of the American Congress in 1776, and compared that with the English Convention of 1688, which had first broken with the Stuarts. This strange linking of a respect for the ghost of the Stuart kings with the rebellion of the American colonists shows the tortuous pattern which was to be borne out later in one of Burns's closest friends, William Maxwell, and after whom his deathbed son was called. In a most extraordinary paradox, this man, whose family, the Maxwells of Kirkconnell, had suffered in fact and not just in fancy for the Stuarts, would form part of the guard that escorted Louis of France to the guillotine. Whether cast as Jacobite or Jacobin, Maxwell knew what it was to be an outsider.

There perhaps lies another clue to Burns's Jacobitism. It was a poetic haven for the educated yet voteless and powerless. It stood not just for a colourful past where Scotland had her place in the sun, but against the grinding orthodoxy of hard-line Calvinism or the suffocating propriety of the Scottish establishment of the day. Added spice was the shadow of sell-out by the ruling interests:

> *What force or guile could not subdue*
> *Thro many warlike ages*
> *Is wrought now by a coward few*
> *For hireling traitor's wages.*
>
> SUCH A PARCEL OF ROGUES IN A NATION

There is a long tradition of Scotland for sale. Even as a child Burns read of it in William Hamilton of Gilbertfield's English translation of Blind Harry's *Wallace*:

> *... then slily on his Hands,*
> *They slipped cunning and most cruel Bands.*
> *Which underneath with sicker Cords they drew,*
> *Alas the* Bruce *that binding sore may rue.*
> *For* Scotland's *Ruin quickly came about,*
> *Occasion'd by the loss of* WALLACE *stout!*

Wallace had fought with a single-minded ferocity to restore the throne to the rightful king. Burns believed in a certain kind of kingship as plainly as Wallace. As 'Scots Wha Hae' expressed so forcefully, he believed that any king should uphold and champion liberty, as he believed Bruce had done. Here is a thread that connects those apparently ill-assorted bedfellows of Jacobitism and interest in revolution.

And at the end of the day what was it that the Covenanters had fought for, and that the Jacobites and the reformers and revolutionaries would all fight for? It was the same: to possess the nation. Burns took the matter and in this case himself no less seriously. He chose as best he could to speak for the nation.

Shamed by a century of wars so barbaric as to defy comprehension, European countries are today very wary of identifying military prowess with national character. Yet as the surviving cult of the Scottish soldier should remind us, it has not always been so. The Scots military tradition is as frightening as Prussia's, and much longer. Nonetheless, there has also been a certain ambivalence about it, and the various ways in which Burns re-flected this are revealing. In his day, a considerable number of Scottish lairds – Highland as well as Lowland – were absentees, serving in either the British army or navy. It was seen as a form of public service, even a burden and duty of gentility. But the combination of poverty and military profes-sionalism had a long pedigree, at least as far back as the days of Joan of Arc. Her triumphal entry into Orléans included a considerable contingent of professional Scots soldiers, and their tune was 'La Marche des soldats écossais'. This is recognisably the same as 'Hey Tutti Tatti' or 'Nou the Day Dawis', and the tune traditionally supposed to have been King Robert the Bruce's march to Bannockburn that Burns used for 'Scots Wha Hae'.

In the early seventeenth century both Scottish individuals and whole regiments played a significant part right from the outset of the Thirty Years War, a conflict that was in European terms the first 'world war' both in its scope and its horror. The Royal Scots, the oldest regiment in the British army, returned from that conflict with 'The Scotch Mairch'. This pipe tune had spread fear across the Low Countries, the Germanies and the Czech Lands by signalling the approach of Scottish soldiery, and it would have been familiar to Burns as 'Dumbarton's Drums'. That same and other Scots regiments were a valuable part of Marlborough's army, and without the initiative of his Scots officers there might have been no victory at Blenheim. The Seven Years War from 1756 to 1763 saw the debut of the first modern Highland regiments in the British army. So effective were they that the government even toyed with the fantastical notion of reintroducing some quasi-clan system in the Highlands to provide a store of martial energy in the service of the nascent British empire:

> *But bring a Scotsman frae his hill,*
> *Clap in his cheek a Highland gill,*
> *Say, such is royal George's will,*
> *And there's the foe!*
> *He has nae thought but how to kill*
> *Twa at a blow.*
>
> THE AUTHOR'S EARNEST CRY AND PRAYER

Burns's *sodgers* with their boozy swagger, tattered uniforms and lack of limbs are usually found at the bottom of the heap. He never condemned the soldier for his trade, for whatever he had been up to, he was also and ever a social victim. The randy soldier is a rascal, but beneath the joke he is also a symbol of virility:

O wha'll mow me now, my jo,
An wha'll mow me now:
A sodger wi his bandileers
Has bang'd my belly fu.
WHA'LL MOW ME NOW?

In fact, Burns's correspondence is frequently laced with military metaphor: artillery, sieges and so on. Two of his sons became professional soldiers. The first two books he read were about warfare: the life of Hannibal and the history of Sir William Wallace. As he told Dr John Moore in his autobiographical letter of 2 August 1787:

Hannibal gave my young ideas such a turn that I used to strut in raptures up and down after the recruiting drum and bagpipe, and wish myself tall enough to be a soldier; while the story of Wallace poured a Scotish prejudice in my veins which will boil along there till the flood-gates of life shut in eternal rest.

The other, more mature, side of his feelings about war was plain enough. Scott remembered when, at Dr Ferguson's house in Sciennes in Edinburgh, Burns noticed the picture of a soldier lying dead in the snow with his miserable dog on one side and his widow with a child in her arms on the other, and remarked that 'he actually shed tears'. Here indeed was 'man's inhumanity to man'. The reference in the picture was to the battle of Minden and the campaigns in the hills of eastern Canada. Both related to the Seven Years War and the growth of empire, 'Scots Wha Hae' also referred to the growth of empire; the military imagery was clear enough – for those who would resist 'proud Edward' II of England 'welcome to your gory bed, or to Victory'. Burns had an insight into the glamour and fascination military trappings have for men, but no illusions about the consequences.

There was nothing glamorous about His Majesty's Excise Service, but it was the nearest Burns ever got to military action. On 29 February 1792 he and other excise officers found themselves wading chest-deep into what would have been the freezing waters of the Solway east of Dumfries, advancing towards the small sailing vessel *Rosamond*. Behind them were the few dragoons they had managed to muster, and before them the vessel grounded on the sands, awaiting the incoming tide to lift her off. The

Rosamond had been involved in smuggling, and the crew blasted away at the advancing party, but with no effect, as they could not bring their guns to bear on them accurately. When the advancing party was getting dangerously close, the smugglers lost their nerve, deserted the vessel and bolted over the Solway sands towards England. Part of the vessel's equipment included four carronades, small and effective snub-nosed cannon then made at the Carron Ironworks, near Falkirk, a place Burns had visited five years before, but to which he had not been able to gain entrance. In the subsequent *roup* or public sale, of the *Rosamond's* contents, Burns bought the guns and sent them to the Legislative Assembly of France. Much has been made of this as an act of revolutionary zeal. In fact, Burns was supporting what at that stage people thought was becoming a constitutional monarchy – like Britain's – against the black reaction of the Austrian empire. The guns never got there, allegedly held up by the customs office in Dover, perhaps for want of payment of the appropriate dues as much as anything. The cost to Burns was between three and four per cent of his income for that year. What was remarkable was not just that he spent the money, but that he had it.

Carronade. It was small and highly lethal guns of this type — turned out at the Carron Ironworks — that Burns sent to France in support of the National Convention.

The Excise Service existed to collect taxes. It was an active life, because the exciseman had to record and measure a considerable range of industrial processes in the area to which he was assigned. In a country area, that could cover hundreds of square miles. A whole range of manufactures were subject to tax, and included basics such as salt, leather, soap, glass, candles, paper, some textiles and of course anything to do with tobacco or alcohol. Some home-made versions of these products were exempt, but generally the excise tax threw its net wide, and to make sure that it was paid accurately, manufacturing processes were measured from raw material to finished product, hence the term *gauger* or measurer. Those products that were imported ready to trade, such as tea and brandy, were also taxed, and part of the gauger's job was detecting the illegal import, or smuggling, of such goods. Hence the *Rosamond* incident, the need for the gauger to go armed on occasion, and Burns's brace of very serviceable pistols. Together with that other main branch of the tax-raising service, the Customs, the Excise was also one of the pillars on which government rested. Without an income, there could be no armed forces and little public administration.

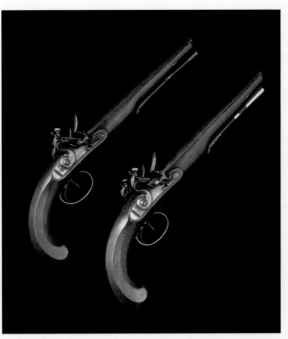

The brace of pistols that Burns had as an exciseman. He probably only carried them when hunting smugglers, who might themselves have been armed.

Because the gauger's job touched a lot of basic trades and activities, the population would happily outwit him at every turn; when they could not do that, his adversaries would hold him in the same derision that the poacher has towards the gamekeeper. On the other hand the government needed the revenue, so great efforts were made to enforce the law by a highly professional service. The backbone of this was a government service that was unusually free from corruption, and that would have been highly attractive to Burns.

Thus he became a *placeman* or salaried servant of the state. He did not fall into this employment casually along the way. It required certain personal qualifications such as a good level of numeracy and sharp powers of observation, and of course a resistance to the temptations that opportunity would certainly offer. As a servant of the Crown the gauger would be expected to show unconditional loyalty to the Crown, swearing in his Oath of Abjuration to accept the king as the legal occupant of the throne, and to defend him personally against 'all traitorous conspiracies and attempts'. There were various hurdles to overcome even to be considered for the Excise Service, including a certificate of suitability from a serving exciseman in a promoted grade and security of two hundred pounds from two sponsors. Because of the financial security the service offered, there were always far more applicants than posts. If an applicant had influence, then by the rules of the late eighteenth century it was standard practice to use it. But no amount of influence would get a candidate into the Excise Service if he were unsuitable, and once in, influence could not get a gauger promotion if he had not earned it.

Burns had thought of a post in the Excise at some point between abandoning an intention to emigrate and his first visit to Edinburgh in

Near the head-waters
of the Ayr at Laigh
Dalfram, where
Burns's friend John
Lapraik farmed.
Beyond lies Muirkirk.
This was the edge of
familiar territory for
Burns, and he passed
this way on his
journey to Edinburgh
in November 1786.

PHOTOS: GAVIN SPROTT

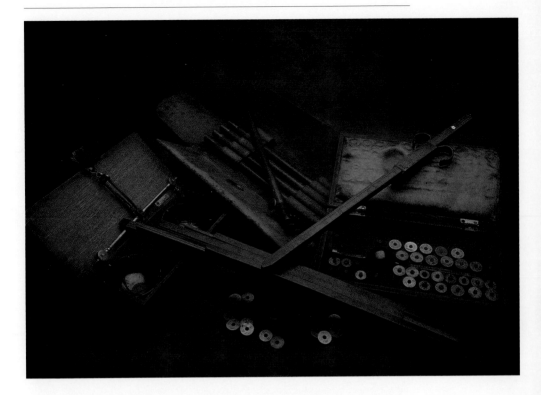

November 1786. He had powerful friends to interest themselves on his behalf, principally James Graham of Fintry, one of the Commissioners of Excise for Scotland, and in the event he needed his friends, not least to save him from himself.

Excise tools and equipment.

One of Burns's eccentricities was to scratch out lines on windows with a diamond-shod stylus that he had been given by the Earl of Glencairn, and as with other serious graffiti artists, these effusions were often the product of impulse or strongly held belief. On his visit to Stirling in 1787 he beheld the wreck of James V's great Renaissance palace, where:

> *... Stewarts once in glory reign'd,*
> *And laws for Scotland's weal ordain'd ...*
>
> *A race outlandish fills their throne:*
> *An idiot race, to honour lost—*
> *Who know them best despise them most.*
>
> WRITTEN BY SOMEBODY ON THE WINDOW

'The Deil's awa wi'
the Exciseman.' The
fun of Burns's song is
captured in this
engraving by C. A.
Doyle, published in
*Poems and Songs of
Robert Burns, with
original illustrations*
(Edinburgh, 1868).

Words, but that was all, for as he also stated, 'the injured Stewart line
is gone'. As we have seen, part of Burns's Jacobitism was the neglect of
Scottish sensibilities. Sir Walter Scott addressed the same question, and
would bring the 'idiot race' to Edinburgh in the person of George IV and
reverse the process.

But however harmless, Burns realised that his lines were hardly flat-
tering to the king whose service he hoped to enter. On a return journey two
months later he smashed the pane. Too late! The lines had been copied and
circulated, and had reached one of the commissioners of the Excise Service

in which Burns was seeking an appointment. As he told Clarinda, in a letter of 27 January 1788: 'I have been question'd like a child about my matters, and blamed and schooled for my Inscription on Stirling window'. Burns had got a reprimand for his behaviour, but was not told that he need no longer apply. The humiliation was enough for him to say that he had 'almost given up the excise idea'. 'Almost' was the important word, because he certainly did not. As we have seen, he was to get further admonitions for what was deemed intemperate language, but in the end it was all irritation at the style of the man who would not bridle his tongue, not at the serious content of his words. If there had been any doubt as to Burns's fundamental reliability as opposed to his Jacobite rhetoric, he would never have seen service in His Majesty's Excise Service, let alone survived in it.

In fact, Burns pushed his case for employment with considerable vigour. Once he had decided to try the farm at Ellisland, he hoped to combine this with excise work, and set about getting appointed to that particular *ride* or area. He even suggested the removal of the current incumbent, who had become 'a wealthy Son of good-fortune' through his wife's inheritance and for whom 'the injury is imaginary'. Indeed, this may well have been the case, but it shows a remarkable persistence on the part of the poet.

And he got his way. But working a farm and riding often thirty or forty miles on four or five days in the week would prove too much, especially in the face of the increasingly common bouts of ill health. The idea of leaving the farm occurred to Burns even before he had got into the stride of his excise duties, but as he confessed to Fintry in a letter of 31 July 1789:

> *The worst of it is, I know that there are some respectable Characters who do me the honor to interest themselves in my welfare & behaviour, and as leaving the farm so soon may have an unsteady, giddy-headed appearance, I had perhaps better lose a little money than hazard such people's esteem.*

Burns was in danger of being trapped in the role of the heaven-taught ploughman. But it was not how he now appeared to those he met. On occasion Burns's excise duties would find him far from home at nightfall, and he would stay with people whom he had got to know in the area. One such host was Andrew Jaffrey, then minister of Ruthwell. His daughter Jean, who was then in her early twenties, left an interesting vignette:

> *Many times I have seen Burns enter my father's dwelling on a cold rainy night, after a long ride over the dreary moors. On such occasions one of*

*the family would help to dismember him of his dreadnought and boots,
while others brought him a pair of slippers and made him a warm dish
of tea.*

Once the poet was comfortable and rested, the household would settle to an evening of enjoyment, Burns reciting some of his poems or singing songs. Jean Jaffrey added that she never could fancy 'that Burns had
ever followed the rustic occupation of the plough, because everything he
said or did had a gracefulness and charm that was in an extraordinary degree engaging'.

Burns's excise duties took him over large tracts of rural Dumfriesshire
with a frequency and thoroughness that nothing else could have done. He
ranged from just north of the Burgh of Dumfries in the south to the foot of
the Dalveen pass in the north and west to the Kircudbrightshire border.
The mounted *gauger* with his folding sliding rule and other instruments
would have been a familiar sight, but not a regular one. Excisemen were
enjoined to make their rounds unpredictable for obvious reasons, and all
the evidence suggests that Burns was good at his job. This is amply borne
out in Graham Smith's most attractive study, *Robert Burns, the Exciseman*
(Darvel, 1989).

As Burns reported to Fintry in a letter of 9 December 1789: 'I dare to
be honest, and I fear no labor'. His life was busy: 'the visits of good angels
[the poetic muses] are short, & far between, but still I meet them now and
then as I jog through the wild hills of Nithsdale'.

He found time enough to laugh at himself in rhyme:

> *Searching auld wives' barrels,*
> *Ochon, the day!*
> *That clarty barm should stain my laurels!*
> *But, what'll ye say?*
> *These movin things ca'd wives an weans*
> *Wad move the very hearts o stanes!*
> ON BEING APPOINTED TO AN EXCISE DIVISION

Burns's excise travels extended something that he had done as soon
as he had money in his pocket after his first Edinburgh visit, and that was
to see other parts of Scotland. His tours took him to the eastern Borders,
through the two northern counties of England, through southern mainland
Argyll, Highland Perthshire and over Drumochter to Inverness, then
eastward through Moray into Buchan, and southward through the land of

his father and cousins in Kincardinshire. There were other less extended expeditions into Stirlingshire and Galloway and incidental journeys to places within a day's ride of Mauchline or Dumfries. The only parts of the Lowlands that Burns never saw was that thin eastern seaboard stretching up to Caithness.

In those parts of the central and eastern Highlands that Burns visited, Gaelic culture is now but a memory, but then it had the appearance of a heartland. 'Ossian' Macpherson came from near Newtonmore. The first Gaelic translation of the New Testament was completed in 1767 by James Stuart, the minister of Killin, with the assistance of the Rannoch poet and schoolmaster Dugald Buchanan. His son John Stuart, also a minister, wrote down the poetry of the great Duncan Bàn MacIntyre, and completed the translation of the Old Testament in 1801. Gaelic medieval musical traditions were carried into the eighteenth century by such long-lived dynasties as the MacGregors of Glenlyon and the Cummings of Strathspey. Although Burns showed little interest in the Gaelic language, the native tunes caught his ear, and he first set 'Ae Fond Kiss' to one of them. He never failed to note 'Highland hospitality' as something special. Before he ever got near the Highlands, he had an image that he conveyed in 'The Jolly Beggars':

> With his philibeg an tartan plaid,
> An guid claymore down by his side,
> The ladies' hearts he did trepan,
> My gallant, braw John Highlandman.

The canine plebeian in 'The Twa Dogs' he names the Gaelic *Luath* or 'Swift', the name a Highland drover might have given his dog, but Luath speaks with an Ayrshire tongue. Similarly, the physical furniture of landscape in Burns's poetry hardly ever deviated from his native south west Lowlands. In his 'Address of Beelzebub' he makes his Scots tongue speak for Highlanders, his barely containable sense of outrage expressed in a lethal irony, the kind of creative discipline he could achieve using his own voice. One might wonder that his visits to Edinburgh and his rambles throughout other parts of Scotland produced none of that vivid sense of place inspired by his own South West, where even his descriptions of the weather are worth a study on their own. In fact, in Burns's journals and descriptions of his travels, there is more comment on the weather of expression and landscape of feature in people's faces than anything else. It would find its mark in Kate in 'Tam o' Shanter', who, 'gathering her brows like gathering storm', is only the most famous example. The Scotland Burns knew may

John Syme (1755–1831), engraved by J. T. Kelley. Along with the poet's physician Dr William Maxwell, Syme, the Collector of Stamps at Dumfries, became a particular friend of Burns after he took up his post as an exciseman in the town. Reproduced from *Land of Burns.*

have been shaped by the land, law and institutions, but for him its spirit was expressed in her people.

Burns had the ability to make new friends right to his final years in Dumfries, while keeping up with his now considerable acquaintance elsewhere with a stream of lively and often revealing letters. Had Burns never written a line of poetry, his letters would have made him a figure of literary interest. They range from a careful formality to a racy freedom of expression that show how articulate he must have been in English as well as Scots.

With his latter-day friends in Dumfries it was different. There was not the same necessity to write, for William Maxwell the doctor stayed in the Burgh and John Syme with his sinecure of the Stamp Office did his business beneath the first house occupied by the Burns family in Dumfries in the Wee Vennel. Maria Riddell stayed out of town, and to her it was usually a brief, often witty and sometimes flirtatious note. The latter was hardly surprising, for she was not only thirteen years younger than Burns, with a natural gaiety and striking beauty, but she also had a cultivated

159

A grace before dinner; Extempore

O, thou, who kindly dost provide
For every creature's want!
We bless thee, God of nature wide,
For all thy goodness lent:
And, if it please thee heavenly guide,
May never worse be sent;
But whether granted or denied
Lord bless us with content!
Amen !!!

intellect. She was English, and, despite her youth, she had travelled, and that would have added an element of novelty and freshness. Another with whom Burns became fast friends was John McMurdo, the Duke of Queensberry's chamberlain at Drumlanrig near the head of Nithsdale, and Burns saw him either as a neighbour at Ellisland, or later on his excise rounds. This set had one thing in common. They were, like McMurdo, rising into a professionalism that equalled gentility, or they were born of established gentry, but, with the exception of Maria Riddell, they had to work for a living, even if, as in Syme's case, their work was not onerous. And though she did not have to work, Maria Riddell was not idle, producing a competent book on the Leeward Islands, where her father had been governor. What Burns discovered here was a circle of people who were educated but without pretension. The men took Burns as he was and shared his enthusiasms. He could over-indulge with them on occasion, even becoming 'a little turbulent', but that did not matter. Maria Riddell had a falling-out with Burns over an incident in her brother-in-law's house at Friars' Carse at which she was not present, but the breach was mended. Now, finally, Burns did not live a kind of double life. He did his excise

A grace before meat and drink was the least a convivial company would expect if the celebrated 'Rhymer Rab' dined in its midst. In her 'Memoir Concerning Burns' of August 1796, Maria Riddell wrote, 'none certainly ever outshone Burns in the charms – the sorcery I would almost call it – of fascinating conversation; the spontaneous eloquence of social argument, or the unstudied poignancy of brilliant repartee'.

Brawliemuir, in the Braes of Glenbervie, Kincardineshire. The *rickil o stanes* in the foreground is said to be all that remains of the house Burns's great-grandfather James and great-grandmother Margaret inhabited. The old road once went near the house, and Burns met some of his cousins here on his return from his Highland tour in 1787. The farm was in the Burness family until 1807.

PHOTO: GAVIN SPROTT

rounds; on occasion he repaired to the Globe to de-
molish some refreshment when friends visited; he
was an assiduous brother at the local Masonic lodge;
and he attended the parish kirk. His educated friends
saw Jean and the children in his home, and the mark
of their regard for them is the effort they made to
provide for them when Burns died.

The most widely read sample of Maria Riddell's
literary skill was her 'Memoir Concerning Burns',
which was published in the *Dumfries Journal* the
month after he died, and was reprinted elsewhere. It
was the best account of his life to appear at that time,
and, as we shall see, one that was soon swamped by
other efforts that were either malicious or incompe-
tent. She started by considering the irreparable loss
of what she described as 'the Caledonian poet'. Af-
ter a vivid description of him as a person and a discussion of his poetry, she
noted with a determined frankness the 'irregularities even of a man of genius', but pointed out that 'the world must have continued very stationary in
its intellectual acquirements, had it never given birth to any but men of
plain sense', and she quoted from 'The Vision':

> But yet the light that led astray
> Was light from Heaven.

She recalled 'the bleak morning of his life' and how beneath Scotland's cold sky 'a genius was ripened without care or culture, that would
have done honour to climes more favourable'.

In his Dumfries years, Burns himself was confident in this position
he had single-handedly created for himself as 'Caledonia's bard'. As he jok-
ingly remarked to John McMurdo in a letter written in July 1793: 'Kings
give Coronets; Alas, I can only bestow a Ballad. – Still however I proudly
claim one superiority even over Monarchs: My presents, so far as I am a
Poet, are the presents of Genius.'

Maria Riddell (1772–
1808) by Sir Thomas
Lawrence. This
young
Englishwoman's
character and
intelligence matched
her beauty. Despite
one period of
estrangement, she
was one of Burns's
firmest friends in
Dumfriesshire, and
following his death
she was loyal to his
family and memory.

CHAPTER SEVEN

A KITTLE MEMORY

Besides writing on windows, Robert Burns had other peculiarities which, had he lived to old age, might have matured into a reputation for eccentricity. Another speciality was writing epitaphs – often for the living. For the most part this was a harmless exercise of wit, but not always. When his pride was injured, Burns could and would sting. He wrote of himself living, sometimes directly, and sometimes as a comic actor in his own creations. He had the Devil dance off with the exciseman: that is, himself. His 'Elegy on the Death of Robert Ruisseaux' is also a sporting reference to himself, *ruisseaux* being the French for streams or burns. It was also apposite:

> *Tho he was bred to kintra-wark,*
> *And counted was baith wight and stark,*
> *Yet that was never Robin's mark*
> *To mak a man;*
> *But tell him, he was learn'd and clark,*
> *Ye roos'd him then!*

Farming and a reputation for strength was all very well, but using his brains and knowledge was what counted for him. This poem was written in 1787. When he was faced with the prospect of death, he was in no such joking mood. He could see it coming. In his last years in Dumfries he was periodically so incapacitated by illness that he could not carry out his excise duties, which by then was a walking circuit through part of the Burgh rather than an arduous rural round on horseback. Returning through the streets to his house one evening he was so immobilised with weakness that two passing women remarked that the poet Burns was drunk. Indeed, he got *fou* on occasion, always as the result of being in a drinking company.

Burns to his father-in-law, James Armour, written on 10 July 1796, just eleven days before
his death. The deterioration in Burns's health is apparent from his handwriting.

NATIONAL LIBRARY OF SCOTLAND: ACC.9381/434

Alexander Cunningham (d. 1812) by Sir Henry Raeburn. Burns revealed much of his attitudes towards love, religion and his general outlook on life to this Edinburgh lawyer. It was an equal friendship, and Cunningham did a lot to raise support for Burns's family when he died.

PRIVATE COLLECTION

On such flimsy foundations would rest the myth of decline and fall that would haunt the biographies for a century.

The reality could not have been more different. Burns's diligence and competence in his excise duties had marked him out for promotion, despite the shadow that had attached to his political views. He attended closely to his children's education, following his father's example. He ensured that his wife had the means to dress fashionably in a time and place where such things were important. When finally he set his hand to the Volunteer movement, he did so with a will and gave character, song – and also moderation – to the proceedings. When death stared him in the face, his concern was not for himself, but the welfare of his family, and the thought that they might be reduced to poverty when he could no longer provide for them.

There was no escape from the heart disease that had dogged him. From January 1796 he was increasingly ill, often unable to rise from his bed. His days were brightened by Jessie Lewars, a neighbour who helped Jean nurse him. She was the pretty daughter and sister of two of Burns's fellow excisemen. Despite his condition, even in these last months and weeks Burns was still writing outstanding poetry. During this time he wrote 'O wert Thou in the Cauld Blast' for Jessie Lewars. Outside, it was a harsh world, the 'hungry gap' of early spring of that year turning into near starvation. He was still labouring at the *Musical Museum*, but only with great effort. As he wrote to Johnson in early June 1796:

> Alas, the hand of pain, & sorrow, & care has these many months lain heavy on me! ... This protracting, slow, consuming illness which hangs over me, will, I doubt much, my ever dear friend, arrest my sun before he has well reached his middle career ...

As spring wore into summer, his doctor friend Maxwell had advised a course of sea-bathing at Brow, a little down the coast from Dumfries. There he went on 3 July. Wading chest high into the cold water must have hastened the outcome, but made no difference to the inevitable. There, at a nearby inn, he met Maria Riddell for what both then realised would be the last time, for Burns could hardly eat, and was reduced to a shadow of his former physique. 'Well, Madam', he said, 'have you any commands for the other world?' Grim reality and grim humour, yet as Maria recorded, all the mental vigour was still there, she 'had seldom seen his mind greater or more collected'. He enquired kindly after herself, for she was also in poor health. Then he spoke plainly of his approaching end, and his fear that 'every scrap of his writing would be revived against him to the injury of his future reputation: that letters and verses written with unguarded and improper freedom ... would be handed about by idle vanity or malevolence, when no dread of his resentment would restrain them'.

On 7 July Burns wrote from Brow to his friend Alexander Cunningham in Edinburgh: 'You actually would not know me if you saw me. – Pale, emaciated, & so feeble as occasionally to need help from my chair – my spirits fled! fled!' While still at Brow, what were perhaps the first flashes of delirium showed in his distressed reaction to a tailor's bill. With difficulty he made it home to Dumfries in a friend's gig. His signature had disintegrated to the near indecipherable. He lapsed into delirium, and at five in the morning on 21 July 1796, life slipped away from him. Even as Jean lay in childbirth, his body was convoyed to the burying ground in what was the most spectacular funeral that Dumfries has ever seen.

Robert Burns did not die penniless or friendless. His library alone was then valued at ninety pounds, at least as much, if not more than what he might earn in a year. His friends, particularly John Syme, William Maxwell and Alexander Cunningham set about making provision for Jean and the family. In the short term they found this quite hard-going, but in the end they succeeded. The cumulative efforts of well-wishers, some of whom had not known Burns personally, and even some who had been the butt of his wit or irritation, such as William Maule of Panmure, meant that the family was not only well provided for, but prosperous livelihoods for the sons ensured. Sir James Shaw, an Ayrshire man who had made good in America, settled in London, and eventually become Lord Mayor of that city in 1805, helped to secure a position for Robert in the Stamp Office in London, and commissions for James and William with the East India Company.

Another Scot with various North American adventures behind him who had settled in England was James Currie. Born at Kirkpatrick Fleming in Dumfriesshire where his father was then minister, Currie was three years older than the poet. He graduated in medicine from Edinburgh University in 1780 and set up as a doctor in Liverpool, prospering enough to buy himself a small estate in his native Dumfriesshire in 1792. As an ardent admirer of Burns's poetry, it was to him that the poet's friends turned to write a biography to raise money for the family. He was hardly well qualified

Burns's funeral
procession, Dumfries,
25 July 1796.
Engraved from a
painting by W. E.
Lockhart.

NATIONAL LIBRARY OF
SCOTLAND: MS.15966.

to do this. He had met the poet once briefly in the street in Dumfries. His
only publication to date had been a report on the effects of water as a cure
for certain ailments, with observations on the effects of opium and alcohol.
He knew something of the latter from his own youth. As a respectable
doctor approaching his middle years, he now trod a path of cautious
propriety. His fear of offending the living made him less than careful of the
memory of the dead. In the event, for the essentially decent, respectable
and mediocre Currie, his own escape from facing ensuing controversy was
a sad one. He died only nine years after the poet, also of heart disease, but
having achieved his main objective – to raise funds for the poet's widow
and children through the publication of his four-volume *Life of Burns* in
1800.

Currie took his cue from Robert Heron, who wrote his *Memoir* of
Burns shortly after his death and had it published first in *The Monthly
Magazine and British Register*; thereafter it was reprinted widely. The son of
a Galloway weaver, Heron had studied at Edinburgh University, and although he became licensed to preach in the Church of Scotland, he never
did so, but made his living through his pen. Heron had first met Burns at

136

Dr Blacklock's house in Edinburgh. The gentle, blind Dr Blacklock had been one of Burns's earliest supporters in the literary world. When Heron visited Burns at Ellisland, he was given a letter to take to take to the old gentleman, but he managed to lose it, sparking off the poet's irritation:

> *The Ill-Thief blaw the Heron south,*
> *And never drink be near his drouth!*

Heron never ranked as a close friend or correspondent. There was something about him that aroused Burns's suspicion. Referring to the lost letter, he surmised:

> *But aiblins, honest Master Heron*
> *Had, at the time, some dainty fair one*
> *To ware his theologic care on …*
> EPISTLE TO DR BLACKLOCK

Heron's partiality to a dram was well known. As the lines indicate, Burns had smelled out some amorous adventure ill-camouflaged by pious cant. Double standards in religionists was something Burns had no time for. Perhaps a hint of Burns's distaste had stung Heron during his brief visit to Ellisland, and with the poet gone, he was free to take his revenge. As the proverb puts it, 'The man that has wrang't ye will nivver forgie ye'.

Heron was for a time assistant to Dr Hugh Blair, minister at the High Kirk of St Giles in Edinburgh, in some minor capacity. Blair had encouraged Burns when he came to Edinburgh, recognising his extraordinary abilities, but for all his intelligence he was a simpering votary of 'good taste', and was ruffled by Burns's *roch* earthiness. This tone is communicated in Heron's *Memoir*, where the word 'peasant' was losing its simple and innocent meaning of a country person or small farmer, and becoming identified with crudity and ignorance. No weaver's son is speaking. Heron assumed the inflated condescension of a man of the world, larded with an air of ingenious knowledge of his subject's psyche. He was in fact a clever, pathetic and unstable rascal who ended his forty-three years sunk in drink and debt.

Currie shied away from too much speculation on Burns's character, but inherited the condescending air which was to irritate Thomas Carlyle so in his famous essay on Burns in the *Edinburgh Review* in 1828: 'He [Currie] everywhere introduces him with a certain patronising, apologetic air; as if the polite public might think it strange and half unwarrantable that he, a man of science, a scholar, and gentleman, should do such honour

Dr James Currie
(1756–1805), first
editor and biographer
of Robert Burns.
Drawing attributed
to Thomas Stothard.

to a rustic'. Currie also took from Heron what may have merely served as a dramatic device: the theme of the flawed genius. Neither Heron nor Currie ever cast doubt on Burns's greatness as a poet. However, they did aver that he drank himself into an early grave, Currie adding hints of venereal disease fuelled by debauchery. Heron spoke of 'the disgrace and wretchedness into which he saw himself rapidly sinking … the sorrow with which his misconduct oppressed the heart of his Jane [sic]'. The tale ends in dramatic style:

At last, crippled, emaciated, having the very power of animation wasted by disease, quite broken-hearted by the sense of his errors, and of the hopeless miseries in which he saw himself and his family depressed; with his soul still tremblingly alive to the sense of shame, and to the love of virtue; yet even in the last feebleness, and amid the last agonies of expiring life, yielding readily to any temptation that offered the semblance of intemperate enjoyment; he died at Dumfries, in the summer of the year 1796.

Other memoirs, particularly that of Maria Riddell, were honest, generous and balanced, yet they did not catch the public eye. Charged with his task, Currie gathered what was available of the poet's papers. Instead of a few scraps he found himself among a disorganised mass. Some papers so shocked him that he burnt them: for instance, a dangerously frank correspondence between Burns and his learned Edinburgh friend William Smellie.

Careless of fact, lacing their work with dramatic half-truths, Heron and Currie started a trend. Others followed with additional and romanticised information, such as Robert Cromek, a Yorkshireman who at least did what Heron and Currie did not, which was follow what might be called the first 'Burns Trail', resulting in his *Reliques of Robert Burns* in 1808, and *Remains of Nithsdale and Galloway Song* in 1810. For some of the latter Cromek got material from 'Honest' Allan Cunningham. The son of one of Burns's neighbours at Ellisland, he was a child of four when the poet arrived and seven when he flitted to Dumfries. This personal connection did not prevent his *Life,* published in 1834, from being full of invention and far from honest. He added freely what he thought the poet ought to have said, but never did.

Of this pair, it might be said that their inventions had a creative aspect. If Cunningham's work floated on a raft of fantasy, it did not give a wildly distorted picture of the character of Burns. Cromek was an engraver to trade. He was evidently a rogue in his financial dealings, which caused Blake and others with whom he had worked to brand him a thief. He was also superb at his craft. The *Illustrations of the Poems of Robert Burns* from designs by T. Stothard was published in 1814, the first of many of its kind. The fine engravings were by Cromek, and clearly show the influence of Blake. Sadly, Cromek had died of tuberculosis at the age of forty-two, two years before this publication.

The stream of inaccuracy continued with John Gibson Lockhart's *Life of Robert Burns*, published in 1828, repeating the theme of the flawed genius, the story careering from an obscure birth through a brilliant apogee to the destined fall. Lockhart had married Sir Walter Scott's daughter Sophia. Perhaps the prestige of this association, and the undoubted accomplishment of his style, lent the effort credence. Then came Carlyle's famous review of Lockhart's *Life*. In fact, after giving Lockhart a metaphorical pat on the back, Carlyle ignored him and launched into the first assessment of Burns's achievement that stepped outside the existing mental tramlines. When Carlyle said that 'a Scottish peasant's life was the meanest and rudest of all lives, till Burns became a poet in it', he spoke from experience, for he was the son of a stone-mason. The rough scenes of country life were 'not seen by him [Burns] in any arcadian illusion, but … the smoke and soil of a too harsh reality [are] still lovely to him'. Carlyle grasped the sheer vitality in Burns: 'And observe with what a fierce prompt force he grasps his subject … three lines from his hand and we have a likeness'. Interestingly, he reckoned that the songs would rank as Burns's greatest achievement. 'They do not *affect* to be set to music, but they actually and in themselves are music'.

Carlyle quarried at what he himself called the inward springs and relations of the man's character, and tried to see him in the context of 'man's existence, with its infinite longings and small acquirings', a turn of phrase that one suspects would have spoken much to the poet. Carlyle felt that, as Burns himself had hinted to Johnson, he had never reached his full potential. He had wanted the leisure and length of life. Carlyle also saw fault in the morality of Burns's life, but his view was not founded on the myth of debauchery, but on an attitude that he detected in the writing, a want of 'a high heroic idea of Religion, of Patriotism, of Heavenly Wisdom'. That

Heron's *Memoir* and Currie's *Life* established the myth of Burns the dissolute drunkard. In this letter of 14 March 1818, Gilbert Burns apologises for a delay in supplying Currie's publishers, Cadell & Davies, with new information he had felt it was his duty to bring to light, 'qualifying the representation of my Brother's moral habits given by Dr Currie'. In fact, Currie's biography was not significantly revised.

NATIONAL LIBRARY OF SCOTLAND: MS.1655.

Bolton Kirkyard, East Lothian, the burying place of Agnes Brown, the poet's mother, Gilbert his brother, and Anabella, his unmarried sister. Despite his eventual modest prosperity as factor to Lady Katherine Blantyre at Grant's Braes, near Haddington, Gilbert's life had not been an easy one. In 1788 Robert saved him from ruin, yet it was years before he won clear of the financial mire. He and his wife Jean Breckenridge buried five of their eleven children here. Gilbert died on 8 April 1827, aged 66.

PHOTO: GAVIN SPROTT

Insert:
Gilbert Burns.
Silhouette, perhaps by Howie, 1816.

Thomas Carlyle
(1795–1881) by
Walter Greaves,
c. 1879. In his 'Essay
On Burns' (1828)
Carlyle was in no
doubt why the appeal
of Burns's writings
would endure: 'The
excellence of Burns is,
indeed, among the
rarest, whether in
poetry, or prose; but,
at the same time, it is
plain and easily
recognised: his
Sincerity, his
indisputable air of
Truth.'

perhaps tells us more about Carlyle than Burns. As a reviewer, he was in no position to question the facts of Burns's latter days as stated, yet he was the first to note that 'we are not medically informed' whether Burns's untimely death was 'an accidental event' or brought on by his way of living.

It was Carlyle's belief that Burns's fame would endure as the personal memory of him faded, as he became 'shorn of that casual radiance'. Gilbert had died in 1827. Of Burns's most faithful friends, Alexander Cunningham had died in 1812, and the 1830s saw most of them disappear. John Syme went in 1831, Jean Armour and William Maxwell in 1834, and Alexander Findlater, Burns's old boss in the Excise Service, who had fought a sterling rearguard action to vindicate the poet's personal reputation, died in 1839. James Grierson, the laird of Dalgoner, was six years older than Burns, and knew him when he was at Ellisland. From 1805 he had been recording the memory of personal details of the poet's life. In 1843 he was gone.

Robert Chambers was the person who took up the challenge to review the poet's life in a fresh perspective. Born in Peebles in 1802, he spent his later schooldays in Edinburgh. When only twenty-one he published his *Traditions of Edinburgh*. Sir Walter Scott was impressed, wondering 'where the boy got all the information'. His range of interests was considerable and mostly historical, but at the core of it was his propensity to ask questions and root about for fresh sources. His interest in customs and song gave him a feel for oral as well as written evidence. His *Life and Works of Robert Burns* was long in preparation, and he was willing to alter it when he came on fresh evidence or research. It was first published in 1851 'after minute personal investigation'.

As Chambers noted in his first line, seven biographies of Burns had already been written. He justified the eighth on the grounds that Currie had been so keen to placate 'so many offended Conventionalities [that had] brooded and whispered over his grave', that although he had achieved his laudable purpose of supporting the widow and family, he had merely arranged others' reminiscences and supplied background information. 'It would even appear that, in his anxiety to avoid provoking any loud demonstration from those who took unfavourable views of the life and conversation of Burns, he had allowed himself – unwittingly, no doubt – to go somewhat beyond the strict truth in his concessions to the imputed faults of the unfortunate Bard'. Nor had Currie attempted to organise Burns's work in a way and sequence that made sense of it, but had confined himself to 'a pure and tasteful selection'. Chambers attempted to dig up the facts. He spoke at length to those surviving, such as Isabella, Burns's youngest sister. Also, he was working in a very different age.

There was visible proof of this. One of the more astonishing events of Jean Armour's widowhood was to see her husband's remains dug up and removed from their kirkyard *lair* in Dumfries nineteen years after his death and reinterred in a magnificent new mausoleum nearby. Her own remains would also be buried there another nineteen years later. On 25 January 1820, after a fundraising campaign by Alexander Boswell of Auchinleck, the foundation stone of the Alloway monument was laid. This edifice alone would cost three thousand and three hundred pounds. In 1831 the statue by Flaxman modelled on Nasmyth's portrait was placed in its monument in Regent Road in Edinburgh. This was hardly the sign of an indifferent public.

Isabella Burns Begg (1771–1858), the poet's youngest sister, by William Bonnar, 1843.
SCOTTISH NATIONAL PORTRAIT GALLERY

The publication of the poems tells its own story. By 1825 they had been printed in fifteen towns in Scotland alone. Over the same period in England they were printed in Alnwick, Newcastle, Durham, York and Liverpool, significantly all in the north, and between 1787 and 1810 there were fourteen editions or impressions in London. In Ireland they were printed in Belfast, with six impressions between 1789 and 1806; in Dublin, with four impressions between 1787 and 1803; and in Cork, in 1804. In the United States they had been printed twice in both Philadelphia and Baltimore.

The return of Burns's son William from India was the occasion of a spectacular gathering in a field near Alloway in 1844. Robert, the eldest son, who had spent years in a fruitless and unhappy clerkship at the Stamp Office in London, his other brother, James, his aunt Isobel, some cousins and Jessie Lewars from Dumfries were all present. Although it was still August the weather was foul, but that did not prevent some eighty thousand people coming from all over the United Kingdom. The Earl of Eglinton said that they had met after a lapse of years 'beneath the Monument which an admiring and repentant people have raised to him' to pay their homage. In reply, Robert spoke for himself and his brothers in pointing out that poetic genius was not hereditary, and that the mantle of Elijah had not descended on Elisha, yet they were conscious of the honour done to them,

Burns came to drink the water at Brow Well nearby, and wade chest-deep into the sea here in a final attempt to restore his health. The strain can only have hastened the inevitable outcome. Burns died within days of leaving here. This shore has been aptly described as Burns's Gethsemane.

PHOTO: GAVIN SPROTT

not just by the illustrious of their own land, but also 'the many generous and kind spirits from other lands – some from the Far West, a country composed of the great and the free', sentiments of which his father would have approved.

So far, all had been brief and to the point. Then Professor John Wilson, the principal organiser of the occasion, got to his feet. Indeed, he praised the bard in the most fulsome terms, but to the point of being carried away by his own eloquence. He spoke for over an hour, and in the course of this ventured on to what was now dangerous ground:

> In speaking of the character of Burns, in the presence of his sons, I must speak reverently; but ... I must not refuse to speak the truth. Burns, like every other mortal being, had his faults – great faults in the eyes of men, and grievous in the eyes of Heaven above ...

Although he went on to extol Burns's achievement, 'there was ex-

144

treme discomfort on the part of many present' at this reference to the supposed vices of the poet.

The first edition of Chambers's *Life* was published in 1851, and reflected this ground-swell of changed opinion. Chambers was also the first
to recognise the universality of Burns. It had been 'long before men could
shake off an idea, derogatory in its general bearing, that Burns was only a
wonderful peasant. He was one of the greatest poetical spirits, without any
regard to the accidental circumstances of birth and education'. Chambers's
achievement would be reinforced by a revision of his work by William
Wallace, published forty-six years later, which incorporated material which
had since come to light, made factual corrections, and, as Wallace himself
put it, stuck to 'the golden Cromwellian rule of biography – warts and all,
but not warts above all'.

Subsequent biographies of Burns were far from uncritical panegyrics,
but according to their various lights they would try to get at the essence of
the man. In 1896 W. E. Henley's *Life* was the last to recycle the flawed

genius thesis in its crude form, and there it was being used as a club to beat what was seen as a slavishly uncritical Burns cult. By then it did not seem relevant.

Thus Burns had been rehabilitated, more than rehabilitated; but it did not merely happen, like some returning tide. It had to be fought for. And for some the tide of reputation had never gone out anyway. Although there is no certainty as to when the first Burns Club was started, it is said that the Greenock Club was active within a decade of the poet's death, as was the Paisley Club. There was a pattern in the Bachelors' Club in Tarbolton. Formed in 1780 with the youthful Burns as its president, it was the unwitting prototype of many of the clubs which would be formed, not just to maintain the poet's memory, but also for discussion and good fellowship. The first *Burns Nicht*, as the celebration of the birthday would come to be known, is said to have taken place on 29 January 1802 at the birthplace in Alloway, now conveniently turned into a public house. They did not keep the 25th until the mistake in Currie's biography was realised later.

Now there developed something like two stories of Burns's life, one from Heron and Currie, and the other an inherited memory among those who had known him personally. Some became the grand old men of the early Burns Clubs: John Syme in the Dumfries Club (1820) and Davie Sillar in the Irvine Club (1826). In 1816 Gilbert Burns and George Thomson figured large in a grand dinner in Edinburgh at which Walter Scott was a moving spirit, and in 1848 a now aged George Thomson participated at the foundation of the Edinburgh Club. John Syme, one of Burns's closest friends in Dumfries, protested roundly that the truth had been abused.

Others would make the same protest, including the quiet Gilbert. The poet's granddaughter Sarah (who was painted with her grandmother Jean Armour) recalled her father James Glencairn's no-nonsense comments: 'My father said it was disgraceful the statements made out by people who lived in the Poet's time, containing as they did, so much falsehood and exaggeration of the events of his life'.

Following the Greenock and Paisley Clubs, the Kilmarnock Club was started in 1808, and one in Dunfermline in 1812. The latter two clubs would have a particularly active role in what would follow. Kilmarnock started early to collect and preserve valuable manuscripts, and was a prime mover in setting up the Burns Federation in 1885, and Dunfermline would initiate competitions among schoolchildren for illustrations of Burns themes.

'The Holy Fair' contains a roll-call of six ministers. In August 1785 they had come to Mauchline from the surrounding parishes to take part in the preparation for the annual sacrament of communion. The main part of this was a series of sermons preached in the open air, the officiating minister standing in the *tent* or open-fronted wooden cabin. Burns did not just criticise the Kirk in some abstract way, but used 'the most deliberate and horrible cruelty and brutality towards the ministers of religion. The worthy clergymen who were gibbeted by this executioner were well known. He takes care to point them out by name'. Thus recalled one of them, the Rev. William Peebles, then minister of Newton-on-Ayr, and twenty-six years later the still enraged author of *Burnomania – The Celebrity of Robert Burns Considered*. Although he reckoned Burns's 'allusions are absurd in the court of poetry as well as abominated in the courts of decency and religion', he finished his tract in triumphant doggerel:

> *Imbibe his spirit, sing his songs,*
> *Extol his name, lament his wrongs,*
> *His death deplore, accuse his fate,*
> *And raise him far above the great.*
>
> *What call you this? Is it Insania?*
> *I'll coin a word, 'tis Burnomania.*
> *His Greenock friends we therefore dub*
> *The Annual Burnomanian Club.*

These 'heralds and followers' of the Greenock and other Burns Clubs alarmed William Peebles, because Burns had not fallen into oblivion. He is still nettled that all those years ago sages such as Blacklock and Blair had given Burns encouragement. He could not think how George Thomson could include the likes of 'Rigs o Barley' and 'Willie Brew'd a Peck o Maut' in his collection. And if he felt such songs were unfit for the eyes of the young ladies who might stumble on them, other poems reduced him to a barely articulate rage. But the burden of his message was that his indignation was not as widely shared as he felt it ought to be. He had 'often been greatly shocked, to hear the names of Hume and Burns mentioned with warmth of applause, by those who are Christians: the one a determined infidel, living and dying: the other an irreligious profligate'. The other associate in iniquity he names, although with no connecting argument, is Tom Paine: 'the lowest of the low, the vilest of the vile'. Others, those of the brutish multitude, are also there by implication. In execrating 'The Whistle' which recorded a drinking contest between two lairds, he comments

147

that had the participants 'been hecklers and ploughmen, porters and chairmen', our wonder had been less.

This seems comical now. In its day it would not have been. There is a grinding logic of assumed moral authority, a merciless dissection of all the inconsistencies between what Burns appeared to be and what he had written. There is also a sweeping dismissal of the notion that Burns was very conscious of his imperfections. And in a perverse way, William Peebles was right. Burns had rejected his moral authority and indeed parts of his morality; he did express an element of agnosticism; he did admire Tom Paine; and he did dare to represent the life and even fun enjoyed by the common people as worth consideration.

Peebles was not a lone voice. Others would come back to the charge repeatedly. Without the sense of personal injury to encumber him, in 1869 the Rev. Fergus Ferguson demanded of the congregation of the East United Presbyterian Church in Dalkeith, 'should Christians commemorate the birthday of Robert Burns?'. Here was not the 'songster' as Peebles had sarcastically referred to the poet, but 'a man of extraordinary mark and significance'. Like Milton's Satan, Burns is set up as an opponent worthy of his metal: 'What is hypocrisy and cant, but to say one thing and to do another: to sneer at proud men, and be as proud as Lucifer one's self ... to shudder in print at seduction, and yet be a seducer: that is what Burns did'. But although Ferguson was also merciless in exposing all Burns's moral inconsistencies, he was not abusive. His final charges were of a philosophical nature: 'We see a great diabolical spirit rising in our midst. It is the deification of mere intellect, genius or force, apart from ... Christian principles'. At the heart of it was 'the worship of humanity for the worship of Christ'. Indeed, the minister may have been correct, but he had missed the point

In his own day Burns hardly bothered to contest such charges. His instinct was to walk away from them with an air of weary *ennui*. He did not so much refuse to conform, for he was in many ways very conventional. Rather, he refused to *obey*. He was not the cool Satan of immorality, but outwardly a walking chaos of moral disorganisation, dodging and mocking the strictures and control of accepted spiritual authority. It was not his unconformity in itself that so disturbed some ministers. Scotland was a grim garden of unconformity, one denomination refusing to conform to the other's notion of the truth, but all within a self-imposed discipline that was often depressingly authoritarian. The enemy was Burns's unruly spirit, all the more so when it continued and burgeoned as a focus of liberation for so many people years after the poet had died.

A disapproval of Burns was shared by many on the evangelical wing of the Church of Scotland. When that element grew into the Free Church at the Disruption in 1843, and eventually a schismatic West Highland and Island 'Wee Free' faction of that body later in the century, it did much to block the popularity of Burns's poetry in these areas.

Behind the fronts of battling spiritual orthodoxies and the cultivated taste of educated society, the Scotland Burns knew was still a rough old place. In fact, that was one of its qualities. Great questions of theology, philosophy, law, science and literature were debated in what had recently been and in many areas still was a poor country. Although this cultural activity was concentrated in the towns, most of the participants had rural roots or connections. Those connections were with what was still most of the population. As we have seen, the numerous small towns and villages of late eighteenth century Scotland existed to serve the countryside with their specialist trades and professions and markets. Scotland was still a rural country. With that went a no-nonsense directness and practicality, a sense of one world. As the *Shorter Catechism* demanded, what is man's chief end? To praise and glorify his maker. However it did not prevent people enjoying life, whether that was social life or relations with the opposite sex.

Sir Walter Scott (1771–1832), drawn by Benjamin William Crombie, *c.* 1831. He never doubted Burns's extraordinary genius, yet harboured cranky reservations about the poetic character of someone who was not reared as a gentleman.
SCOTTISH NATIONAL PORTRAIT GALLERY

By the middle of the following century Scotland had become a very different place. Several big events had been part of this change. The long slog of the French wars, only ending with the defeat of Napoleon at Waterloo in 1815, had created the first popular sense of solidarity with other parts of the United Kingdom (although people, including Sir Walter Scott, still referred to them as the United Kingdoms). If southern nationalists still obdurately referred to the state as England, in Scotland there was an increasing sense of Britishness, and even the conversion of Scotland into North Britain. But that conversion was a confident one. Scott was not the 'Wizard of the North' for nothing. For Scott, the loss of statehood in 1707, and the debacle of the mostly Scottish rising against the house of Hanover in 1745 were sacrifices and defeats out of which he conjured the phoenix of a triumphant Scottish identity. Highland and Lowland identities were conflated in a sea of tartanry that Burns would have found distinctly *agley*.

If George IV's visit to Edinburgh in 1822 and Victoria and Albert raising their standard at Balmoral in 1848 marked a national integration of Britain on one level, the Reform Acts of 1832 and 1833 were both a beginning on another. In many ways, the Reform Acts marked the real Act of Union between Scotland and England, for much of the ancient – and cheerfully corrupt – fabric of the old Scottish local government was swept away, and a revitalised British Parliament was born with a law-making appetite that would break down many of the distinctions between Scotland and other parts of the United Kingdom.

Against this background Scotland was changing fast, even just to look at. The Highlands were already on the *via dolorosa* of the clearance of whole populations from the interior glens to the coasts to make way for sheep, and in 1845 came the dreadful potato famines and further clearance, this time to the Lowland towns and beyond. In the Lowlands it was a different story. The Agricultural Revolution was modernising the last of the unimproved landscapes, as in Buchan and Easter Ross. There would be decades of sustained prosperity which would be remembered as the time of 'high farming'. The railways came, the Central Belt became the 'Workshop of the World', and Glasgow the Second City of the British Empire. The Bard might be as popular as ever, but the world he knew was increasingly seen through a glass darkly.

A simple measure of this is the way in which his poetry was illustrated. One of many examples is the painting by Gourlay Steell engraved by John Le Conte and published probably in the 1840s. It shows a thoughtful poet standing by his plough contemplating a disconsolate and homeless mouse. Not only are the details of the plough, horses and working arrangement totally wrong, but, most telling of all, Burns is depicted as working in the clothes he wore in the drawing-rooms of Edinburgh. Alternatively, the readership increasingly needs to be transported back to another world. Chambers' and Wilson's *The Land of Burns*, published in 1840, was illustrated with scenes showing rural activity by D. O. Hill.

It was not just time but social change that was carrying another generation away from that world. We have already seen the rags-to-riches story of Elizabeth McGuire. The Tennant family with whom she was associated, the progeny of William Burnes's friend 'Guid Auld Glen' also rose into property and titles, but not through a fluke of wealth. They had to work for it. Charles Tennant, 'Glen's' fourth son by his second wife, was born in 1768. He became a weaver in Kilbarchan, and by experiment he developed a bleaching powder by 1800. What had before taken a year now took a few days. By the time Charles died in 1838, his St Rollox Chemical Works in Springburn, Glasgow, was world famous. His grandson, also Charles, became a baronet, and the next generation was raised to the peerage. This was the Victorian fairy tale where virtue was industry and was also rewarded. Holy Willie's god who sends one to Heaven and ten to Hell, according to some mysterious logic known only to himself, had become a memory. Predestination had been trampled underfoot by the cult of self-help preached by Samuel Smiles. In the life of every great man might lie a parable of justification by good works, and in the sober success of countless thousands was written the virtue of unrestrained work and a very restrained appetite for anything else. How would the spirit of Robert Burns be interpreted according to the lights of what was a very different age?

Robert Chambers, with his historian's ability to see the past in terms of its own values, remarked that 'with a strange contradiction to the grave and religious character of the Scottish people, they possessed a wonderful quantity of indecorous traditionary verse, not of an inflammatory character, but simply expressive of a profound sense of the ludicrous in connection with the sexual affections'. His older contemporary Professor John Wilson had no time for this indulgent view. It was not a matter of different generations, but a fit subject for a bourgeois cultural *jihad* against the excesses of the rabble, against 'the ribald wit and coarse humour of some of the worst old ballads current among the lower orders of the people, of whom the moral and religious are often tolerant of indecencies to a strange degree'. Those worst old ballads were, of course, exemplified in the *Merry Muses of Caledonia*. Burns had made a systematic collection of bawdy songs, and a version of this had found its way into clandestine print four years after his death, and thereafter enjoyed a secret circulation. One subtitle cautioned that it should not be seen by 'maidens, ministers or striplings'.

That was not to be the case. One minister to see the *Merry Muses* was George Gilfillan. Such was the esteem in which he was held by his Dundee congregation that they named a church in his memory. He was evidently a man of considerable and indeed headstrong character. He was also a great Burns enthusiast, thus the discovery of the *Merry Muses* posed a perplexing problem for him. But he did not flinch from the path of duty. In the biography published as part of *The National Burns* in 1878 he recalls how in 1872 he had gone through the book with a friend, Robert White: 'Deep sorrow, rather than anger, was in our hearts as we went over it together'. But he had known what to expect, for in 1847 he had, in *Hogg's Instructor*, written how, in his last days in Dumfries, Burns 'was desperately at bay, vomiting forth obscenity, blasphemy, fierce ribaldry, and invective. Alas!

the mouth which once chanted 'The Cotter's Saturday Night' on the Sabbath day ... was now an open sepulchre, full of uncleanness and death ... a hideous compost of filth and fire'. He blamed not the Devil as such: rather it was 'that raging animalism, which was too often prominent, came here to its height'. This theory was confirmed at the time he and Robert White had gone through the *Merry Muses*. His friend had retailed the account of an innkeeper – Gilfillan could not remember his name – whose home Burns had frequented. The poet had been 'most delightful society, but beyond that he would often spend the rest of the evening in singing obscene songs: at a certain stage the poet and the man were spirited away ... the Brute only remained'.

Gilfillan was sure that Burns must have been drunk when he compiled the *Merry Muses*. The demon drink was his downfall, but it was only a race between that and another dark hand. The poet had reeled out of the Globe Tavern and into a house of ill fame:

> *... and there behaved so disgracefully, being of course intoxicated, that he was spurned out, and fell into a hedge opposite the door. The ground was covered with snow, and when he awoke and went home, he found the fatal chill and the accidental disease to boot.*

The late Dr William Anderson of Glasgow 'appeared to have this on good authority'. Accidental disease! This circumlocution for a venereal infection is wonderful indeed, and we may now laugh at George Gilfillan for his painful credulity and foolish assertion. Yet, as with the charges of his fellow ministers, although the above assertions were nonsense, the central burden of his complaint owed something to reality. Burns might not have been flattered by the description of 'animalism' on its own, but he would have owned it as an acceptable part of human nature. As the subscript to the title page of the 1800 *Merry Muses* said:

> *Say, Puritan, can it be wrong*
> *To dress plain truth in witty song?*

For respectable Victorians, the answer was yes, but they also had a powerful alternative.

'Highland Mary' was one of Burns's most celebrated loves. On a miserable November day in 1920 a posse of local dignitaries and Burnsians watched a team of workmen dig up her grave in Greenock. The location was a badly run-down area near a local shipbuilder's yard that had amalgamated with

Harland and Wolff. With all the sunken war-time ton-
nage to replace, they needed to expand, and the old burying ground had to go. Not without a fight, because this
disturbance of the remains of 'Highland Mary' had provoked fierce opposition among the Burnsian community.
However, the remains were reburied at another Greenock
cemetery a few days later with many beautiful floral trib-
utes. That would have been the end of the matter, but for
the report on the exhumation in the *Greenock Telegraph*
nearly two months later. There had been an infant's coffin
found beside the adult remains. No one thought this worthy of note at the time, but the matter exploded into a
bitter controversy ten years later when Catherine Carswell
made a simple assertion of death in childbirth in her fresh
biography of Burns. Had 'Highland Mary' indeed died in
a typhus epidemic, heroically nursing her brother, who
had recovered, or had she died giving birth to a child gotten
on her by Robert Burns? The very thought of this
unchastity quite enraged the 'Mariolaters' as they were
called.

A madonna-like
nineteenth-century
figurine of Highland
Mary in Dunfermline
Public Library.

FIFE COUNCIL.
PHOTO: GAVIN SPROTT

　　The 'Highland Mary' of the poems was in fact not
Mary at all, but Margaret Campbell, who was born at
Auchamore near Dunoon, Argyll, on 18 March 1766. This, and what can
be pieced together about her relationship with Burns, is just one of the
many intriguing points of detective scholarship in Dr James Mackay's 1992
Biography of Robert Burns. She was the eldest child born to Archibald
Campbell and Agnes Campbell. While still a girl of twelve Margaret was
working at the manse in Lochranza in Arran. In 1785 she was a nursemaid
at the house of Gavin Hamilton, Burns's lawyer friend in Mauchline. Both
before and after that she was byre-woman at the nearby Coilsfield House.
In the spring of 1786, when she was still at Coilsfield, she and Burns became intimate. The nature and degree of that intimacy will never be known.
There are several poetical references to 'Highland Mary', the most famous
of which is 'Thou Lingering Star':

> *Eternity cannot efface*
> *Those records dear of transports past,*
> *Thy image at our last embrace –*
> *Ah! little thought we 'twas our last!*

　　Although hardly among the greatest of Burns's works, written in a stylised Augustan English, the poem still trembles with a distracted pain at something that went wrong. It describes his last day with 'Highland Mary':

> *The flowers sprang wanton to be prest,*
> *The birds sang love on every spray,*
> *Till too, too soon, the glowing west,*
> *Proclaim'd the speed of winged day.*

Despite the poems, Burns said little about his relationship with Margaret Campbell. The bare, ascertainable facts are that Burns took up with Margaret after a rebuff from Jean Armour, or, more particularly, from her family. At the time, he was still considering emigrating to the West Indies to escape the mess he had got himself into with Jean. He gave Margaret a two-volume Bible, Old and New Testament, now preserved at the Burns Cottage museum at Alloway. In the front of the second volume is written in Burns's hand 'Thou shalt not forswear thyself, but shalt perform unto the Lord thine oaths' (Matt.V.33).

The presumption was that this was a token of Burns's promise to make a new life with Margaret Campbell in Jamaica.

> *Will ye go to the Indies, my Mary,*
> *And leave auld Scotia's shore?*
> *Will ye go to the Indies, my Mary,*
> *Across th' Atlantic's roar?*
>
> WILL YE GO TO THE INDIES, MY MARY

This continues with the lovers parting to put their various affairs in order before making their way thither. In his *Reliques* of 1808 Cromek got this story rolling in grand style:

> *This adieu was performed with all those simple and striking ceremonials, which rustic sentiment has devised to prolong tender emotions, and to inspire awe. The lovers stood on each side of a purling brook – they laved their hands in the limpid stream – and holding a Bible between them, pronounced their vows to be faithful to each other. They parted – never to meet again.*

Indeed, they did not, for Margaret died a few months later in Greenock.

Grierson of Dalgoner, the note-taking laird, spoke to people who suggested that she had been the mistress of one of the brothers of the Earl of Eglinton. That, as Dr Mackay points out, would not make her into a harlot. By the custom of the day, the attentions of a great man would have been difficult for a servant-girl to resist.

There is also a suggestion that Margaret herself may have been difficult to resist. She appears to have been medium to tall in height, with a fine figure, a profusion of fair hair touched with red, a pretty face and striking blue eyes. She commonly went barefoot and with bare arms, perhaps reflecting her different cultural background, for her mother tongue was not Scots but Gaelic.

It was not long before the public fell for her. Picking up Cromek's fanciful description, Mrs Jameson, in *The Romance of Biography* subtitled *Memoirs of Women Loved and Celebrated by Poets* (1829) lighted on 'Highland Mary': 'Mary Campbell was a poor peasant-girl … who could not write at all – who walked barefoot to that meeting on the banks of the Ayr … Helen of Greece and the Carthage Queen are not more surely immortalised than this plebian girl'. By comparison the other loves of Burns 'are not very interesting or reputable. *The lassie wi the lint white locks* … was an erring sister, who shall be suffered to fall into a shadow'. Clarinda was also real, 'and I am afraid, a person of the same description'. With all such unsuitable candidates out of the way, it was a short step from a 'pure' romance to a spiritual dimension, where Mary is seen as a redeemer in a wicked world. Burns's own poem, 'Thou lingering Star' became known by a name he had never given it: 'To Mary in Heaven'. As late as 1921 Charles Brodie could write in the Burns Chronicle 'At Mary's Shrine':

> *Still in these changed, distracted days,*
> *When olden faiths depart,*
> *Thy love, a constant power, prevails,*
> *And stays the troubled heart.*

Not poetry to the dismissive taste of the late twentieth century. Is this a touching expression of naïve but heartfelt sentiment, or is it sentimentality? In the 1860s W. H. Midwood painted his *Burns and Highland Mary at Failford*. No matter that they would have needed arms twenty foot long to communicate across the water! The kneeling Burns – watched by his suitably impressed collie – reaches over the burn proffering the sacred text. But the focus is on Mary, the barefoot, bare-armed *heilan' lass*, but with her head modestly covered, her gaze directed into her lover's eyes over the black book above which her hand is hovering. It is a scene of sanctified rapture, purged of that dreadful *animalism*, the demon that lurked in wait for the Victorian soul.

Robert Burns and
Highland Mary by
Thomas Faed.
Research by James
Mackay has revealed
that 'Highland Mary'
was in fact Margaret
Campbell, who was
born in Dunoon in
1766, and died and
was buried at
Greenock in 1786.
Faed's was not the
only picture to be
founded on a myth.

CHAPTER EIGHT

SHOULD AULD ACQUAINTANCE BE FORGOT?

Midwood's painting of *Burns and Highland Mary* was only one of various portrayals of this scene. Thomas Faed was more sure-footed, not just in the technical detail, but in his psychology. He abandons bibles and promises and limpid streams, and poses a question. The two lovers are seated side by side. Burns is earnest and persuasive, his eyes and brow lost in Mary's shadow. The sun falls on his lips, and what are they saying? Mary is a mid-Victorian beauty, with her black hair, broad brow, straight nose and small neat mouth. We do not see her eyes, for they are cast down. She is thoughtful and a trifle confused. Her arms are stretched down and away from her lover, her hands clasped in an enigmatic *Angst*. What is going on?

Faed's *Highland Mary* in Glasgow's Kelvingrove Gallery is unusual among Burns illustrations. Most such pictures are straight illustration, faithful to a particular point in the text, and some indeed remarkably faithful. The illustrations of 'Tam o' Shanter' by Thomas Faed's brother John are well known and often reproduced to this day, and understandably so, because they are confident in their detail and catch the character of the tale with a vigorous directness: 'Nursing her wrath … The Souter tauld his queerest stories … Nae man can tether time or tide … And vow! Tam saw an unco sight!' In the latter not only Tam, for the lissome Nanny is revealed in a daring show of flesh that must have sent the odd bead of sweat down a few Victorian brows. The accomplished engraving by Lumb Stocks was published by the Royal Association for Promoting Fine Arts in Scotland in 1855.

The Faed brothers and a considerable variety of artists illustrated a range of favourite scenes such as 'The Cotter's Saturday Night', 'The Jolly Beggars', 'To a Mouse', 'John Anderson My Jo', and of course 'Auld Lang Syne' and other songs. As the century wore on the presses pounded out the poems and sketch versions of Burns's life, the illustrations sometimes cobbled together as in Gilfillan's *National Burns.* Most capable artists turned to other subjects.

Among the exceptions was Sam Bough, who illustrated William Scott Douglas's six-volume *Works of Robert Burns,* published between 1877 and 1879. He moved back to illustrating the context, the best-known example being his painting of the snow-covered Alloway cottage. Bough was a genial no-nonsense Cumbrian with a blunt turn of phrase, an encyclopedic memory and an enthusiastic knowledge of Burns, most of which he could recite by heart. Sydney Gilpin's *Sam Bough RSA* (1905) records an interesting incident at an elevated Edinburgh party in 1856, when he shocked a group of ministers by declaring:

> *God once sent a man into Scotland to show the nation how a purely natural man acted and thought ... This was Robert Burns ... But the professors of piety in the land could not or would not understand the clear-sighted, candid, open-hearted type of man, set up as a beacon before them, and did nothing but revile and persecute him.*

Although several of the ministers lost their tempers under this provocation, history does not relate whether it was Bough's view of Burns or of themselves that they disagreed with. For despite the rearguard actions that we have seen of the Rev. Fergus Ferguson and his like, the weight of respectable public opinion was now overwhelmingly on Burns's side.

There is a particular race of paintings dating from just before the middle of last century until the 1880s, such as William Borthwick Johnstone's *Burns in Sibbald's Library,* Charles Martin Hardie's *Burns in Edinburgh* and *Burns at Sciennes,* James Edgar's *Burns in the Home of James Burnett, Lord Monboddo,* and Stewart Watson's *Inauguration of Robert Burns.* These all show Burns surrounded and admired by the great and the famous, being the focus of attention and completely in command. Such paintings were done in the correct expectation that they would be reproduced and widely distributed as household icons.

In a similar vein the testimonials of eminent men were carefully collected and stacked like so many candles at the shrine. 'Not Latimer, not Luther, struck more telling blows against false theology than did this brave singer. The "Declaration of Independence" and the "Marseillaise" are not more weighty documents in the history of freedom than the songs of Burns', said Ralph Waldo Emerson. 'The books that have most influenced me are Coleridge and Keats in my youth, Burns as I grew older and wiser', intoned

The Burns statue in Leith by D.W. Stevenson, 1898

PHOTO: GAVIN SPROTT

John Ruskin. Such sentiments – indeed a very whiskery male performance – could be multiplied many times. In his own eulogy on 'the great democrat who, proclaiming the Royalty of Man, struck down Rank with one hand and the old hard theology with the other', Andrew Carnegie declared that 'there cannot be too many statues erected to the memory of Burns'. He saw to it that all the public libraries that he funded in the United States had sculptures of the Bard, with the result that they outnumbered the public effigies of Washington and Lincoln.

The earliest sculpted likenesses were *The Muse of Poetry discovering Burns at the Plough* by Peter Turnerelli, which was installed in the Mausoleum at Dumfries in 1819 (restored by Herman Cawthra in 1936), and the Flaxman statue already mentioned. The story of the latter shows how attitudes towards Burns changed over the middle of the century. Flaxman died in 1826 before he had finished the job, and his brother-in-law and pupil Joseph Denman completed it, and it was installed in its housing on the Calton Hill in Edinburgh in 1839. In 1844 it was removed and re-erected in the library at Edinburgh University, where it could be seen to better advantage. But Principal Lee did not think much of having a statue of a non-university man there, and in 1861 it was removed to the National Gallery of Scotland in Princes Street, and thence to its present home in the Scottish National Portrait Gallery in Queen Street in 1889, where by that time it had become a prized exhibit.

It was in the 1870s that the population of Burns statues began to grow, with one in Glasgow's George Square in 1877 and one in Kilmarnock in 1879. The following year a statue by Sir John Steell was placed in Central Park, New York, the first of many erected by ex-patriate Scots in North America and Australasia. The Thames Embankment (London), Dundee and Dunedin statues were all derived from the Central Park one, which, like the Flaxman statue, was based on the head in the first Nasmyth portrait. This was the likeness which dominated, and in some cases it developed a kind of stereotyped vacancy, as in Amelia Hill's statue in the centre of Dumfries. A more imaginative approach developed, as with George Lawson's statue in Ayr, completed in 1891, where the standing figure with his crossed arms and what is almost a pensive scowl give the impression of mental power uncluttered by the props of ploughs and *gowans* and mice. The same may be said for James Pittendreigh Macgillivray's statue in Irvine, which with its broad massy features conveys the same impression of power and energy. They perhaps reflect the reputed judgement of Burns's sister Isabella that the Nasmyth portrait was like her brother, 'but just too pretty'.

Some of the statues of Burns were the result of private benefaction, but most were erected by public subscription, often stimulated by local Burns Clubs. Such communal acts are a very powerful statement, for they indicate a public and not just a personal acceptance. Despots often erect public statues of themselves as a way of pressing acceptance on their subjects, and, conversely, they are usually the first objects to be destroyed once people have freedom. Like the bones of the saints, statues are removed, hidden and reinstated according to the ebb and flow of events. Such was the fate of the Burns statue at the Sorbonne during the Nazi occupation of Paris.

The people who erected statues to Burns in the colonies readily identified him with the British Empire.

> *Burns is one of the assets of the Empire. The love of Burns and his inspiring verses is one of those unseen bonds that bind together the British Federation of freedom-loving peoples ... [T]he soul-stirring strains of his democratic song, 'A Man's a Man, for a' that,' do they not express the very spirit that moves in the breast of the enterprising emigrant and the persevering colonist? Wherever Scotsmen have gone – to the Far West or to the Far South – they have carried with them two books – the Holy Bible and the Poems of Robert Burns.*

This was the view of A. C. White, recorded in the *Burns Chronicle* in 1915, during the Great War. Burns was also an unwitting conscript to that conflict, seen as standing for the opposite to Prussian militarism. The universality of Burns was making him all things to all men, producing some strange contrasts. Otto von Bismarck, the conservative Prussian *Junker* who created modern Germany, was enjoying an evening picnic with friends. When a chill air descended, he first indicated his affection for his future wife Johanna von Puttkamer as he fastened a cloak about her and recited 'O, wert thou in the cauld blast'. Karl Leibknecht, who tried to spread the Bolshevik revolution to Germany, was murdered by a gang of *Freikorps* or proto-Nazi thugs. Reputedly he recited part of 'A Man's a Man for a' that' in their faces before they laid into him with their rifle-butts.

The Burns Federation – a world-wide association of Burns Clubs – was founded in 1885, and one honorary president was Archibald Primrose, 5th Earl of Rosebery. He was active in politics and served in Gladstone's government on and off for many years, becoming prime minister himself for a year in 1894. He wrote books, his horses won the Derby three times and his marriage to a rich heiress completed the picture of a glamorous life. Despite all this, Rosebery found time to take a prominent part in public life in Scotland. He was involved at the unveiling of several of the Burns statues at that period. He also led the public ceremony to mark the centenary of the poet's death in Dumfries on 21 July 1896.

There had been nothing like it since Burns had been laid to rest. Work stopped for the entire population, and by nine in the morning the streets of the town were densely crowded. The procession assembled on the White Sands, and finally got going at twenty past eleven. It included between three and four thousand people, at least eighteen bands, civic dignitaries from all over the south west of Scotland, various local trades, and of course representatives of numerous Burns Clubs from the Burntisland Locomotive Club to delegates from Texas and all over the Empire. It included between seventy and eighty carriages, vans and lorries, and took an hour to pass by.

Archibald Philip Primrose, 5th Earl of Rosebery (1847–1929), by an unknown artist. Foreign Secretary 1886, 1892–4; Prime Minister 1894–5. Rosebery's genuine respect for Burns showed in the way he improved housing conditions for farmworkers on his own estates.

Lord Rosebery was at the Mausoleum, where he was handed the various wreaths to lay over the remains. Then as many as could get in went to the Drill Hall to hear what he had to say. It was a thoughtful speech, pointing out that one hardly *celebrated* the death of a great poet, but 'the coming of these figures is silent, it is their passing that we know'. He spoke with feeling of the struggle of Burns's last months, and his posthumous fame, and to loud cheers from the audience, how Burns 'has become the champion and patron saint of democracy; he bears the banner of the essential equality of man'.

Then Lord Rosebery went by special train to Glasgow, and addressed what was obviously a very grand meeting in the St Andrew's Hall, where he enlarged on the same theme. Where had Burns come from? he asked. 'Try and reconstruct Burns as he was. A peasant, born in a cottage that no sanitary inspector in these days would tolerate for a moment …'. He returned to the theme of the home later, how Burns 'recognised it as the basis of all society … for he knew, as few knew, how unpretentiously but how sincerely, the family in the cottage is welded by mutual love and esteem'. He recalled how Dugald Stewart had walked out with the poet one morning, and Burns had diverted Stewart's rapture over a fine view to the sight of so many cottages with their smoking chimneys, and 'the happiness and worth which they contained'.

As a landowner, Rosebery possessed estates which were the workplace of hundreds of farm servants, most of them living in the tied cottages that went with the farms he rented out. In the late nineteenth century, such rural housing was often wretched beyond belief, and made worse by economic depression. It was frequently damp beyond remedy, cold, there was often a tramp of over a hundred yards to get water from a well that might dry up in summer, and no sanitary facilities at all. For the most part the workers accepted these conditions as life. Despite the pious pronouncements of many prominent landowners that something must be done, Rosebery was one of the very few who systematically rebuilt the housing with such unheard-of luxuries as flushing WCs. It is fair to assume some connection between Rosebery's enthusiasm for Burns and these good works.

A direct connection between Burns and social need was the Cottage Homes erected by public subscription beside the National Burns Memorial at Mauchline and opened in 1898. These provided much-needed housing for retired people, and continue in this laudable service to this day. There was no overt political agenda here, and in his Glasgow speech Lord Rosebery also tried to keep that at bay by making fun of politicians at his own expense. ' "A Man's a man for a' that" is not politics,' he continued, 'it is the assertion of the rights of humanity in a sense far wider than politics. It erects all mankind, it is the charter of its self-respect'. This most distinguished of Liberal politicians would be proved wrong about the politics, and right about self-respect.

Individual poems as much as certain poets come and go in popularity. Such is the case of 'The Cotter's Saturday Night'. In an unpious age, which has grown away from the setting and attitudes of the time when it was written, it can appear to us sentimental and a trifle artificial, whereas the rip-roaring fun and action portrayed in 'Tam o' Shanter' we can fully appreciate. Life in the late twentieth century is not as in Sydney Scroggie's jingle:

> *The grave Victorian, who kept*
> *The Holy Bible where he slept:*
> *Says family prayers, which God enjoys*
> *And daily flogs his little boys.*

Despite the fact that 'Tam o' Shanter' is a cautionary tale, the picture of drunkenness it conveys is not the horrifying deterrent that would serve the purposes of the Temperance movement, battling as it was with a serious social problem. On the other hand 'The Cotter's Saturday Night' was immensely popular, and not just because of religious sentiment. The poem

opens with a direct quotation from Thomas Gray's 'Elegy written in a
Country Churchyard':

> *Let not Ambition mock their useful toil,*
> *Their homely joys, and destiny obscure;*
> *Nor Grandeur hear with a disdainful smile,*
> *The short and simple annals of the poor.*

Burns then shadows Gray in the opening scene, both in metre and
subject, but with a difference, for where Gray paints an effective picture of
a countryside closing down at dusk, leaving 'the world to darkness and to
me', Burns stays with it, getting under the skin of a familiar scene:

> *November chill blaws loud wi angry sugh;*
> *The short'ning winter-day is near a close;*
> *The miry beasts retreating frae the pleugh;*

The Cotter's Saturday
Night, engraved from
a painting by John
Faed. Scenes from
Burns painted by the
Faed brothers were
popular as household
prints in the
Victorian period.
Despite careful
research, the Faeds,
like other artists
illustrating Burns,
sometimes depicted
their own very
different era instead.
Reproduced from *The
Cottar's Saturday
Night* (1853).

The black'ning trains o craws to their repose:
The toil-worn Cotter frae his labour goes, –
This night his weekly moil is at an end,
Collects his spades, his mattocks, and his hoes,
Hoping the morn in ease and rest to spend,
And weary, o'er the moor, his course does hameward bend.

From that point, Burns and Gray diverge on to separate tracks. Gray considers the burying ground:

Each in his narrow cell for ever laid,
The rude Forefathers of the hamlet sleep.

Meditating on their lives, he imagines all the might-have-beens:

Perhaps in this neglected spot is laid
Some heart once pregnant with celestial fire;
Hands, that the rod of empire might have sway'd,
Or wak'd to ecstasy the living lyre.

But Knowledge to their eyes her ample page
Rich with the spoils of time did ne'er unroll:
Chill Penury repress'd their noble rage,
And froze the genial current of the soul.

On one level Burns agreed with that, otherwise he would not have quoted Gray. Yet he takes the theme by the neck and revolutionises it. He stays in the land of the living. He creates a family, from the 'expectant wee-things' that greet their homecoming father, the smiling wife and then the elder children and a daughter's boy-friend who drop in. They enjoy their meal then they turn to family worship. In reading from the New Testament the father pointedly touches on:

How He, who bore in Heaven the second name,
Had not on earth whereon to lay His head …

It is a picture of people who are sane, articulate, dignified and at ease with themselves, and, in the things that matter, they are educated. And who is Burns describing? The landless labouring poor. All Gray's might-have-beens are irrelevant. Life holds out no prospect of material improvement for these people. That is the way they are, but in terms of spiritual development there is nothing to add:

> *Princes and lords are but the breath of kings,*
> *'An honest man's the noblest work of God'*

Burns also touched on the same people in 'The Twa Dogs'. Luath acquaints Caesar, the gentleman's dog, with a different world:

> *A cotter howkin in a sheugh,*
> *Wi dirty stanes biggin a dyke,*
> *Baring a quarry, an sic like;*
> *Himsel, a wife, he thus sustains,*
> *A smytrie o wee duddie weans ...*

Yet these people are not ground down in hopelessness:

> *They're no sae wretched's ane wad think:*
> *Tho constantly on poortith's brink,*
> *They're sae accustom'd wi the sight,*
> *The view o't gies them little fright.*

Despite this, they have the ability to enjoy themselves. 'Bleak-fac'd Hallowmass' is a time for fun:

> *Love blinks, Wit slaps, an social Mirth*
> *Forgets there's Care upo the earth.*

But the threat of ruin is always there:

> *There's monie a creditable stock*
> *O decent, honest, fawsont folk,*
> *Are riven out baith root an branch,*
> *Some rascal's pridefu greed to quench...*

'The Twa Dogs' is the ample political footnote to 'The Cotter's Saturday Night'. Taken together, the two poems are an extremely powerful statement of the dignity of labour. To the late eighteenth century, it was a startlingly new way of looking at the social order. The God of the Covenants might be no respecter of rank, but that was only relevant when he came to

James Keir Hardie (1856–1915) addressing an anti-war meeting, about 1914. Born illegitimate and brought up by his mother, Hardie looked to Burns as his spiritual father, drawing moral courage from his example.

'dicht the corn fae the caff' in the hereafter. In some cases there may have been a feudal familiarity between laird and common people, like Udny and his fool. But in the Lowlands in particular, being poor was to be part of a multitude which educated people either despised or patronised. A patronising attitude was acceptable then in a way quite impossible now, partly because of the change in attitudes that Burns initiated. If Gray checked the attitude of 'grandeur' towards the poor, Burns gave them cause to walk tall in the land of the living.

This translated directly into the growth of popular politics, from Chartism through to the founding of the Independent Labour Party in 1893. One of the founders was James Keir Hardie. Born near Holytown in Lanarkshire in 1856, he was brought up by his mother. Hardie acknowledged the poet as his spiritual father, claiming that 'I owe more to Burns than any man, living or dead'. He worked from the age of eight, and was in the mines from the age of ten, getting fired later for organising his fellow miners. He studied at night school, moved to Cumnock in Ayrshire and turned to the pen for his living. In 1892 he was elected to Parliament for West Ham South, and later represented the Welsh mining area of Merthyr from 1900 to 1915. He guided the young Labour Party on to the course that would make it the main alternative to the Conservative Party in British politics. Hardie was one of that noble breed of nineteenth-century Christian socialists for whom the dignity of labour was the ideal that drove them. This was a factor in Burns's immense and enduring popularity not just in other parts of the United Kingdom, but in altogether foreign cultures.

A down-to-earth contrast to such earnest concerns was William and Andrew Smith's boxworks in Mauchline. In Burns's time the Smith family had made razor hones in the locality. In the 1840s they had a thriving snuff-box manufactory in Mauchline employing about sixty people working ten hours a day six days a week. Twenty years before there had been about fifty similar works in the west of Scotland, many of them in Ayrshire. But snuff was going out of fashion, and many of these works had closed down, leaving the field clearer for the Smith firm. The answer had been to diversify: first into tea caddies and cigar cases, then a wide range of containers useful for keeping the various nick-nacks used in sewing and dressmaking – pirns for thread, needles, darning blocks, thimbles, shears and so on. The range expanded through egg-cups and napkin rings to paper-knives, postage-stamp boxes and inkwells, buttons and badges, to name but a few. By the 1860s, the number employed at Mauchline had increased to over six hundred, and even though similar items were made on a smaller scale elsewhere, the goods were generally known as 'Mauchline Ware'. The products were hand-decorated at first, then transfers and tartan patterns were introduced, and eventually photographs. Although the products were produced as souvenirs for just about every popular location in Scotland and many in England, one of the core markets was items associated with Burns – locations, characters and of course the Nasmyth bust in perfect miniature. Timber from Nanse Tinnock's *howff,* timber from Gavin Hamilton's office and garden, timber from the old couples of Mossgiel farmhouse, even (it was claimed) timber from the poet's coffin purloined when his remains were dug up and removed to the Mausoleum in 1815, it was all pressed into service, wood of the True Cross. Even the living vegetation from around the various Burns sites was stripped and processed.

These products were but part of the industry. Potteries turned out figurines, pitchers, wall or rack plates depicting Tam o' Shanter and Souter Johnny, Tam pursued over the brig by Nannie, Burns and Highland Mary, John Anderson and his wife, Burns by himself, statues of Burns, scenes from the poet's life and death.

Postcard by Donald McGill, reprinted in *The Deltiology of Robert Burns* by Peter J. Westwood (Dumfries,1994). If the lighter side of Burns nowadays sometimes wilts under the weight of scholarly attention, that is perhaps because there have been brief periods when little more was associated with the name 'Robert Burns' than pawky humour and sentimentality.

MR PETER J. WESTWOOD

"SHOULD AULD ACQUAINTANCE BE FORGOT?"

Foundries produced cast-iron effigies of the poet at the plough, which could decorate a hearth or hold a door open, and heads of Tam and Johnny that looked like painted neeps. The invention of the postcard at the end of the last century sowed a bumper crop of curious and entertaining Burnsiana that has recently been harvested in *The Deltiology of Robert Burns: The Story of the Life and Works of Robert Burns illustrated with over 420 different Postcards* (1994) by Peter J. Westwood. James Mackay's *Burnsiana* (1988) amply illustrates what was now a vast and thriving Burns industry.

Burns was a national hero; he was a national possession; and he was a national investment. It was worldly fact as well as lofty sentiment when Lord Rosebery said 'His true life began with his death'. This 'true life' was separated from all inconvenient memories of the flesh. 'With the body passed all that was gross or impure – the clear spirit stood revealed, and soared at once to its accepted place among the fixed stars in the firmament of the rare immortals [loud and prolonged cheering].' Reviewing the extensive Centenary Burns Exhibition in Glasgow in the 1897 *Burns Chronicle*, a member of the Burns Federation reinforced this ascension in vigorous terms:

> *We must have no more apologies for Burns, no more whining regrets anent his lapses and his shortcomings … If Burns had been different from what he was he would not have been Burns. We can always find ready to our hand presidents of young men's Christian associations …*

Quite so. In fact, a certain George Macfarlane was a well-to-do Glasgow merchant who was president and a founder member of the Young Men's Christian Association. Over thirty years later his daughter would write yet another biography of Burns, but it would please neither those unfurling the moral banners of youth nor the now mighty Burnsian establishment. Shortly after the publication of her *Life of Robert Burns* in 1930, Catherine Carswell got a communication through the post. She was urged to use the enclosed 'in a quiet corner and leave the world a better and cleaner place' signed 'Holy Willy'. The enclosed was a bullet. What dreadful deed had she done?

Catherine Carswell was born in 1879 and brought up in Victorian Glasgow, and she paints an interesting picture of her childhood in her autobiography *Lying Awake*. She died in 1946 and it was published posthumously in 1950. Her family lived in a substantial house not far from Sauchiehall Street, but beyond was a tide of slum dwellings that crept ever closer. That did not upset her parents, for they were good Christian soldiers who would march towards the sound of spiritual gunfire. (Both Carswell's minister grandfathers had 'come out' in the Disruption of the Church of Scotland in 1843, a distinction not unlike being an Old Communist in the Soviet Union.) 'We were… a simple and Philistine family' well read in the Bible and a few major classics, but with no interest in the arts. Her parents were sincere and kindly, her father a religious intellectual, her mother other-worldly, both of them strenuous in their efforts to help the poor. For all the affectionate memory she had of her parents as people, Carswell found her upbringing emotionally stultifying. She recalled on one occasion passing through the Trongate with her father on Saturday night about 1890. The drunkenness had assumed an epic quality. 'The spectacle was shocking. But it had a sordid splendour, a whole-hearted, ruinous contempt … I breathed more easily … than when joining in the … hymns at a meeting of the Grove Street Institute (my father presiding) or at a "Happy Sunday Afternoon" for the Canal Boatmen.'

Catherine Carswell (1879–1946), who turned Burns into a Lawrentian hero beating a track to freedom out of stultifying conventionality.

MR JOHN CARSWELL

Catherine Carswell followed her own odyssey away from this upbringing, proving herself to be a person of some courage and determination. She studied music for two years at Frankfurt; she completed the classes in English Literature at Glasgow University, but could not graduate because she was a woman. Her marriage of 1904 was annulled after her husband turned out to be insane. She worked as a reviewer and drama critic for the *Glasgow Herald*, continuing in journalism when she moved to London in 1912, marrying Donald Carswell, a fellow journalist in 1915. Also in London in 1914 she met D. H. Lawrence, and it was the start of a lifelong friendship. It was he who encouraged her to complete her first novel, *Open the Door!*, which was published to some acclaim in 1920. There was a strong element of autobiography, with the heroine, Joanna Bannerman, beating a trail out of a puritanical childhood. The father portrayed is not Carswell's own father, but a man of a 'guarded sunlit emptiness', which is perhaps why she kills him off early in the book, but not before laying the charge that he failed in one essential duty to his wife: 'In the intimate chamber of their married life she was never really awakened'.

But the mother's daughter, who is the heroine, gets there: 'There on the moor that vibrated with noon-day, he was Adam to her Eve ... the past was shed from both of them like a garment'. And with this went the dangerous discovery that evil as much as good had made her 'alive ... an individual ... a divine creation herself capable of creative life'. Another novel, *The Camomile*, followed in 1922. This also was an exodus to the promised land of emotional freedom and self-fulfilment.

Her *Life of Robert Burns* took five years to write. She found it an exhausting task, but also 'definitely ... life-giving in the strangest of ways'. Again, she was strongly encouraged by Lawrence. He had a personal interest in the project, as he had made the beginnings of a fictionalised Burns biography himself but had not continued with it. He urged her to get at the 'real' man inside. There was a vision here of which she spoke in her letters to her friend Florence McNeill, how 'each soul must cut some time or other the umbilical chord and stand up in its essential integrity ... independent of heredity, nation, accident and all else'. It was 'a necessary rebirth, the breaking free, the proud arising of the new naked soul from the morass with the declaration – *here I am!*' In applying this to Burns, she concluded that 'all men of genius in this world are innocents abroad. Innocence, of course, does not exclude wickedness. It excludes only fundamental sophistication, and – though I may be wrong in this, fundamental narcissism'.

Later, scholars would refer wryly to 'Mrs Carswell's romantic biography', and it all seems tame enough now. But in the early 1930s Scotland was a third-unemployed and a half-fed nation of lapsing Calvinists, or even Calvinist atheists. Between the demands of flesh and the destination of soul, that sensitive middle ground of emotional need and personal realisation familiar today was largely *terra incognita*. Passages of the book were serialised in the *Daily Record* before publication, but the reaction must have been unnerving – calls for a boycott, claims that it degraded womanhood, and even covert attempts to get the book withdrawn from publication. Carswell stuck to her guns. She got support from some interesting quarters, including the then little-known Hugh MacDiarmid (Christopher Grieve); she also had encouraging letters from ordinary readers, and the fuss subsided. She was the first to write of Burns within the framework of a popular psychology that we now take for granted.

She did this by trying to piece together the motivations from the evidence, then let a kind of mental movie camera roll through the eyes of the participants. The book has the filmic quality of 'being there'. For instance, at the time of William Burnes's death and Elizabeth Paton's conception:

It was a busy day for Agnes [Robert's mother]. She had now to prepare a substantial meal for the faithful hungry ones who should later return from the graveside ... Lizzie Paton was sick and looking blue beneath the eyes. Her mistress knew well enough what ailed the girl. She hoped that her husband had died without knowing anything ... Such things come to pass, and they are vexing. But Robin was a good hearted lad.

The very use of first names and pet names gives the reader a front seat. But in the event, Robin was not the good-hearted lad his mother thought:

He was sorry for Lizzie, but his sorrow, though sincere, was superficial. The nature of his feelings appears most truly in the jovial and graceless 'Welcome to his Bastart Wean' composed a few months later.

Was it graceless or not? That depends on the motivation, but that was not Carswell's only concern:

Any notion of Robert as a dreamy-eyed young man weaving rhymes while loitering behind the plough, is as prettified as his portraits. An unwelcome energy informed his speech and his movements. Into his Freemasonry, his friendships and loves, he poured the full violence of living.

By the 1930s this 'full violence of living' now included sex. It was of course tastefully conveyed, between the boards of moral, if still novel, respectability in Marie Stopes's *Married Love* (1918), or wrapped in the escapist romance of Hollywood, or leaking half-cooked into the public mind as the 'discoveries' of Professor Freud and his disciples. In the April sunshine Robert takes a good look at Jean for the first time:

She had a pleasant square face, small square hands and frank, widely opened, desirous eyes ... Her bare legs were strong and shapely, her feet remarkably small. She was as shy and as bold as a blackbird.

When it came to Highland Mary, then the fox was really among the hens. On the rebound from his first failed relationship with Jean, Robert is shown as both an innocent and a predator. 'Never was a young man more dangerous to women, never women more necessary to a young man'.

Jean had been willing with the homely and hearty willingness of a young heifer. But Mary was wilder, gentler in her yielding ... Would she marry

him he asked? Seeing him tender and sincere, she said she would ... they
loved without reserve. Before May was well advanced Mary knew that
in due time she would bear Robert a child.

This blew the fuses of the Burnsian establishment. What evidence
did she have? In truth, nothing that would stand up to examination. But
would it have been out of character? One person whose good opinion
Carswell particularly valued was Professor DeLancey Ferguson, of the
Western Reserve University in the United States, a first-rate Burns scholar
as we shall see. As Carswell related with relief to her friend Florence McNeill,
Professor Ferguson had read three-quarters of the manuscript, and thought
it 'gives a juster view of Burns' character and temperament than has been
written yet', but nevertheless 'I don't think he really approves of my *method*'.

The problem with Carswell's 'method' was that, in charting the feelings
and reactions of the *dramatis personae*, she was working as an author does
in a novel. She was constructing an equation in which the interaction of
the characters has to balance if it is going to make sense. Personalities have
to fit, little can be left hanging unexplained. 'There has been knot after
knot to untie all along my way, and I *would not* go on till I had done my
best with each'. Where no hard evidence existed, she would infer it, or rely
on 'local traditions', which are themselves often generated by a dislike of
uncertainty.

In this scheme Burns's periodic fits of depression are acknowledged
but not really faced, even although the poet faced them himself on various
occasions, floored by what he repeatedly called his 'hypochondriac
imagination'. There would be scope enough for others to tackle this and
other aspects later. As Carswell said of the five excerpts in the *Daily Record*,
'I'm so glad of the chance to get at the common reader for whom the book
is fundamentally intended'. She had interpreted events that were now a
hundred and fifty years old in the language of the twentieth century and to
people who knew little or nothing about the times or life that Burns was
born into.

Others would follow, using dramatisation to increasing effect. One of
the best known is James Barke. He was born in Kincardine in west Fife in
1905. Barke's parents were farm servants who had moved from Galloway
via the Borders. On leaving school, Barke went to work in the Glasgow
ship yards, where he became an engineer. However, his main interest was
writing, and *The World His Pillow*, published in 1933, was the first of many
novels. By far the most striking is *The Land of the Leal*, which drew heavily
on his family experience of the land, but ended with a grim foretaste of the

horrors of fascism before it was generally understood. Thus, as with Lewis Grassic Gibbon's *Scots Quair* trilogy, there was the same pattern of movement from country to town complete with an underlying socialist rationale. In 1946 it appeared that he had gone off on another tack. *The Wind that Shakes the Barley* was the first of the five *Immortal Memory* sequence of novels that dramatised Burns's life, and *Bonnie Jean*, about the life of Jean Armour, appeared in 1959, the year after Barke's death. The Burns novels did not carry the same punch as *The Land of the Leal* because Barke was writing his story into borrowed clothes. Sometimes the text can fall back into description rather than live on the tongues of the characters. Yet the sense of the poet as the inspired tribune of the people is strong, and would have struck a familiar note in the Britain that was trying to pick itself up from Hitler's War in a new beginning of social reform. Despite Barke's careful research, it is possible to find deficiencies of fact and oddities of language on most pages of his Burns books, but that would be to miss a simple point: he brought the Burns story to a wide readership that otherwise would have known little about the man beyond the common catch-phrases.

Barke's initial interest had been in the theatre, and it was the failure of the earlier drama movement that turned him to the novel. It was an actor rather than playwright who achieved success here. John Cairney first appeared as Burns in a minor television sketch he did with Jimmy Logan in 1960, and from that grew the idea for the one-man show which first astonished a small audience at the then little-known Traverse Theatre at the 1965 Edinburgh Festival. It is all related with humorous modesty in Cairney's *The man who played Robert Burns* (1987). This would later reach a mass audience on television, but as Cairney recalls, it was taking the show round Scotland live that he came on surprises, as in the Whitehall Theatre in Dundee:

> *Walking through the audience at one point, encouraging them to sing, a pure soprano sailed above the rest from somewhere in the middle stalls. It belonged to fifteen-year-old Elaine Ness, a local girl who was there with her mother ... I only knew that I must use that voice at some point. And that point came just before the death. When 'John Anderson, my Jo John' came up in the script, I indicated to Elaine that she should sing it, and the innocent simplicity of her tongue gave the song all the performance it required and the moment was sealed in the dying fall of the scene.*

Cairney also recalled his visit to a mental hospital, where at first he did not understand the indifferent and knowing welcome he got from the patients.

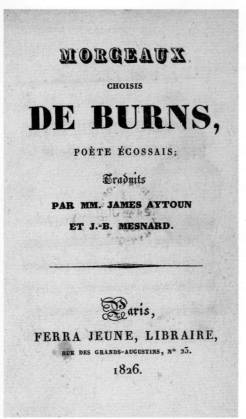

MORCEAUX

CHOISIS

DE BURNS,

POÈTE ÉCOSSAIS;

Traduits

PAR MM. JAMES AYTOUN

ET J.-B. MESNARD.

Paris,

FERRA JEUNE, LIBRAIRE,

RUE DES GRANDS-AUGUSTINS, N° 23.

1826.

The first translation of poetry by Burns into a foreign language, by James Aytoun and J. B. Mesnard, was published in Paris in 1826.

NATIONAL LIBRARY OF SCOTLAND

Passing by an open window on his departure, he overheard one say to another, 'They've took away that man that thought he was Robert Burns!'. Yet for a whole generation of Scots people, he undoubtedly *was* Robert Burns.

Another strand in the Burns legacy goes back to 1791, when the poet was very much alive. That year a dictionary of living British authors *(Das gelehrte England, oder Lexicon der jetzlebenden Schriftsteller)* was published in Berlin, edited by Jeremias David Reuss. Burns's reputation must have been established quickly to generate that kind of notice. Copies of the poems which were printed in Britain were evidently in circulation, because when Thomas Carlyle sent a copy of his *Essay on Burns* to Johann von Goethe in or shortly after 1828, with a suggestion that the great German writer might not have heard of Burns, it turned out that he was wrong: 'I am sufficiently acquainted with [Burns] to prize him'. However, Carlyle's *Essay* seems to have awakened a fresh interest in Goethe. He was born ten years before Burns and would live to eighty-three. He could thus look back and draw his own comparisons and conclusions. His own songs remained in the realm of high art, and 'perhaps one or another of them may be sung by a pretty girl to the piano', but which of his songs 'lives among us that it greets us from the mouth of the people', like those of Burns? In the event Goethe was being over modest about himself, yet he had grasped one of the essential qualities of Burns. Not only the poems but the understanding had travelled.

One aid to a literal understanding would have been Robert Motherby's *Pocket Dictionary of the Scottish Idiom,* published in Königsberg in 1826. This was intended to promote the understanding of the works of Ramsay, Burns and Scott, and included notes on Scottish manners and traditions. The words were given both German and English translations. No doubt Motherby had been able to quarry in John Jamieson's *Etymological Dictionary of the Scottish Language* first published in 1808. A selection of poems was published in Germany in 1832, and the complete poems in 1835, fulfilling 'the wish of our late prince poet [Goethe] to usher into Germany one of the finest poets of the last century'. The first translation, by Philip Kaufmann, followed in 1839. By all accounts, that first was not the best of renderings, but better ones soon followed.

There may have been a similar pattern in France, in that the poems circulated in the original long before finding a translator. *Morceaux choisis de Robert Burns* translated by J. Aytoun and J. B. Mesnard appeared in Paris in 1826, and the first complete works in 1843. In 1896 William Jacks produced a fascinating survey of various translations to date, *Robert Burns in other tongues*. This covered fifteen living languages, and it is interesting that he rates very highly the translations into less prominent tongues, such as Swiss German and Czech, The 1892 translation into English he does not notice. This century would see a further dozen tongues to add to the list, and a fresh Russian rendering by Samuel Marshak in 1950, which would attract great praise. The translations into Japanese by Tameji Nakamura in 1934 and into Chinese in 1990 would prove to be immensely popular.

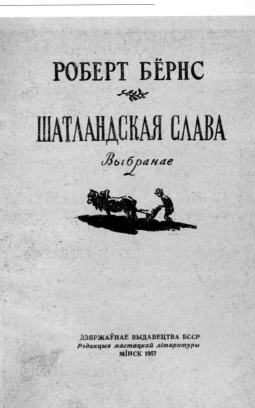

A Byelorussian edition of Burns, published in Minsk in 1957.

NATIONAL LIBRARY OF SCOTLAND

Jack noted two fundamentally different approaches as exemplified by the German and French translations. The former strove to shadow the rhythm and meaning as closely as the German tongue admitted, the French attempted a poetic paraphrase of the meaning that conveyed the essential character, but often abandoned the rhythm. A recent French selection (*Robert Burns: Poésies*, Jean-Claude Crapoulet, Paris, 1994) not only indicates the difficulties of translation, but demonstrates the compact nature of Scots. For instance 'Sweet fruit o' mony a merry dint' becomes the verbal traffic jam of 'De nombreux doux combats tu es le tendre fruit'. On the other hand, the very verbosity of the French can convey a kind of grandeur as in 'Scots Wha Hae':

Ecossais, qui avez, avec Wallace, versé votre sang;
Ecossais que Bruce a menés au combat si souvent;

Allez! La couche sanglante vous attend,
Ou bien la victoire!

'Auld Lang Syne' perhaps fares best of all:

Faut-il nos vieux amis quitter
N'y plus jamais penser?
Faut-il nos vieux amis quitter,
Et tout le temps passé?

Et tout le temps passé, m'ami
Et tout le temps passé,
Buvons un coup à l'amitié,
En souvenir du temps passé.

Bogged down in either incorrigible moralising or uncritical 'Burnomania', Scotland was to reap a better harvest from all this international interest than she deserved. In 1893 the Frenchman Auguste Angellier published his study of Burns, in the first volume, *La Vie* (The Life), and in the second, *Les Oeuvres* (The Works). To this task he brought an understanding of Western literature as a whole combined with a reasonably accurate picture of the Scotland that Burns knew based on personal investigation, and not least an acute mind alert to the foibles of human nature, and a heart-felt agreement with the values that Burns championed. Of 'The Cotter's Saturday Night' he says:

Never has so much dignity been shed on the life of the poor ... And what is admirable in this picture is that this nobility emerges gradually from the reality, surmounts it, conquers it, and finally subdues it by bearing it along in triumph. The piece, which opens with an almost sombre picture of wearied toil, ends in a glorious idea.

Of Burns as the poet of love, his insight has yet to be bettered:

It is the common foundation of desire, that which is primordial, primitive, essential in all loves: pure passion, without idea, without cloud, naked as a kiss.

'Nue comme un baiser!' One cannot but think that Burns himself would have been moved rather than flattered by such praise. There was also a decided shift in emphasis away from moralising or exonerating. Answering his own question as to why he should seek to add to the biographies in English, he concluded that:

it is still possible to shed light on some of the inner workings of his life … Without doubt a secret sympathy for this unusual and brave soul has been a hidden incentive.

Angellier recognised both the usefulness of psychological insight and the subjective element in biography.

Others were also on the trail, including Hans Hecht, professor of English at Basle and then Göttingen Universities. In 1919 he published his *Robert Burns: Leben und Wirken des schottischen Volksdichters* (Robert Burns: the Man and his Work). It was translated into English by Jane Lymburn in 1936. In 1904 Hecht had published an edition of songs with an introduction and notes from the same manuscripts of David Herd's that Burns had drawn on. He travelled much in Scotland as Angellier had done. His *Life* was an honest account, getting to the point and generous in its attitude to the poet, but Hecht was unlucky in various ways. His initial publication was forestalled by the Great War, and the translation into English has a bumpy feel to it; and although he tried to update it to take into account of the research that had taken place in the interval, it was still the last of the old-fashioned biographies of Burns. Worthy and scrupulously scholarly, it lacked the dramatic sparkle of Carswell without adding to the fresh tracks opened up by Angellier. Nor was there a place for an honest biographer of Burns in Hitler's Reich: Hecht was driven from his country.

In 1931 a friendly letter appeared in the *Burns Chronicle*. It informed readers that the study of Burns was now part of the graduate school curriculum of Northwestern University in Illinois, that there was a good interest among the students, and if any Scottish Burnsians were passing by what was a pleasant suburb of Chicago, would they call in 'and let us share their enthusiasm for Burns'. The author was Franklyn Snyder, professor of English. The following year his *Life of Robert Burns* was published.

Like some film directors, Snyder made a discreet appearance in his creation. In describing the Mauchline of Burns, he compares it fleetingly with the village he must have visited, and what was evidently a pleasant encounter with the local *polisman* who guided him and his car to a safe parking place 'sae that yin o thae busses winna tak a wheel aff ye while ye're lookin about'. 'Lookin about' indicates a sharp ear for detail. Not a few

Lochlie, where
William Burnes and
his family farmed.
The house has since
had another storey
added and the
steadings have been
totally rebuilt,
complete with
modern slurry tank.

PHOTO: GAVIN SPROTT

Inset:
Mossgiel today.
Surely the bard would
have approved!
Potatoes – for which
Ayrshire would be
justly famous – were
just becoming a field
crop as part of
eighteenth-century
farming
improvement, and
William Burnes
started growing them
at Mount Oliphant.
Agnes, Robert's
mother, used to peel
the potatoes at
Mossgiel. One of the
few recorded
occasions when
Robert quite lost his
temper was when one
of the workers at
Ellisland did not cut
the potatoes small
enough, with the
danger that the beasts
might choke on
them.
PHOTOS: GAVIN SPROTT

non-Scots speakers would have recorded that as 'looking around'. This same attention to detail combined with a confident clarity produced the first really passable account of the poet's life.

Two recent events had a considerable bearing on Snyder's sure-footed achievement. The first was the publication in 1926 of Sir James Crichton-Browne's *Burns from a New Point of View*. Despite the evidence gathered over a century before from those who had known Burns in his Dumfries days that he was not a drunkard, the biographers had ignored it. Now for the first time a medical man brought up the heavy artillery. Crichton-Browne sifted the evidence, deduced that Burns had suffered from rheumatic endocarditis, and exploded the myth. The importance of this lay not so much in a vindication of Burns's character, but a true understanding of it. Burns's last years were not ones of mental and spiritual disintegration but of a man stopped in his prime.

The other element was a fresh command of the primary evidence. For instance Snyder had the wit not just to repeat the titles of the books that Burns was known to have read in his youth as others had done, but to read them and see what they had revealed to the budding poet. John Ray's *Wisdom of God manifested in the Works of the Creation* (1691) contained an interesting description of a louse, which had an instinct bestowed by the divinity to seek out people with foul clothes 'and provoke them to cleanness and neatness'. Hence:

> *Ha! whare ye gaun' ye crowlin ferlie?*
> *Your impudence protects you sairly;*
> *I canna say but ye strunt rarely*
> *Owre gauze and lace …*
> TO A LOUSE

Snyder's achievement was also the result of a partnership. A fellow American academic at Western Reserve University, John DeLancey Ferguson, had provided him with more primary evidence in a newly-edited pre-publication text of all Burns's letters he could find, and, if Snyder's acknowledgement is to be taken at face value, invaluable guidance: 'Only he and I will ever know how much I owe him!'. DeLancey Ferguson was Snyder's 'unfailing court of final appeal in disputed or debatable matters'. DeLancey Ferguson's edition of Burns's letters was published in 1931. Some years before he had been asked to oversee a new edition of selected poems. Then he knew little about Burns, and was shocked by the lack of reliable information. He had 'everything to learn, but nothing to unlearn'. He started burrowing, checking off hitherto accepted versions against a sight of the originals wherever possible. He uncovered a trail of censorship and deceit. In 1938 the *Burns Chronicle* carried a severe editorial entitled 'Private and Confidential':

> *The decencies of ordinary life must be observed. Those literary hikers who clamber over fences and pluck what they will, regardless of plain notices that they are on private ground, have much to learn of the ethics of biography.*

Perhaps that is why the *Chronicle* never noticed DeLancey Ferguson's edition of Burns's letters, nor *Pride and Passion*, his book on Burns published in 1939. This was not a biography – he thought there had been too many – but an investigation into 'what sort of man was Robert Burns?'. His complaint was that 'somehow the personality which blazes in the poems and glows in the letters only smoulders in the biographies'. He considered that the biographers were too taken up with moralising and the places where Burns had lived, 'instead of the things he did and thought'. DeLancy Ferguson wrote with a detachment and dry humour that was quite Scottish. For instance in discussing whether Burns was carrying on with Highland Mary at the same time as Jean Armour, he commented, 'most biographers incline to the sequel theory on the naïve assumption that love affairs, unlike electric batteries, are always mounted in series and never in parallel'. He was not roused to indignation by the distorted stories of Burns *the drouth*. He observed quietly that if Burns were a drunkard, 'he managed somehow to do it without heavy expenditure, an art few people have ever learned'.

DeLancey Ferguson would get another handsome acknowledgement in 1950, when David Daiches, in his *Robert Burns*, praised the man 'whose noble edition of Burns's letters, to say nothing of his other work in the field, put Burns studies on a new footing'. Thus it is to Burns's international appeal that we have to look for the genesis of our modern understanding of him. Nor did this paradox end with French, German and American scholarship. Professor David Daiches taught at Chicago and Cornell Universities, and he may be fairly credited with reseeding the intelligent study of Burns in Scotland. Further, as he recalls in his autobiographical *Two Worlds* (1956), he was the inheritor of two ancient cultural traditions, those of Scotland and Judaism. With his love of the rich store of human anecdote and wisdom of the Old Testament, Burns would surely have seen something in that.

The moors and hills
of eastern Ayrshire
and northern
Dumfriesshire.
Burns's poetry
developed to express
great ideas, yet his
physical imagery
remained rooted in
his native South West
Scotland, where he
was born and died.

PHOTO: GAVIN SPROTT

CONCLUSION

THE LAST HALF CENTURY has seen many interesting accounts of Burns, and the trans-Atlantic connection established by Franklyn Snyder and John DeLancey Ferguson has continued to be fruitful. In Scotland writers such as Maurice Lindsay and James Mackay have never lost sight of the vital interest and tradition that lie beyond the seminar rooms of universities. This fascination culminated recently in Dr James Mackay's biography of Burns, which went more than the extra mile in verifying facts from original sources and spreading the evidence copiously before the reader. Yet when Snyder recognised that there were many aspects concerning Burns which still baffled him, he realised also that 'it must have been far more bewildering to his contemporaries, no one of whom seems actually to have understood him'. There are many sides to Burns that are unknowable and will remain so. His mystery is part of his attraction.

Surprisingly, understanding of the historical background to Burns is still limited. Theology for instance is not of the same absorbing interest today as it was to Burns's generation, so the all-important strands are not run to ground. Because Freemasonry has since become more of a private organisation, and no longer has the public face of street processions and ceremonies that it once had, it is rashly assumed to be and have been no more than a handy network for self-promotion, thus underestimating the movement's intellectual and spiritual appeal. Scottish constitutional history in its European context is a subject that students of Burns ignore at their peril. Knowledge of the physical cradle of Burns's experience on those now-distant farmlands of Ayrshire and Dumfriesshire varies from poor to distorted. The fact is that there are still many rigs to plough.

Does this continual quest for more knowledge matter? In Scotland we have a living tradition of poetry, ballad and song, which understanding

Royal Mail stamp issue commemorating the Burns bicentenary, 1996.

can reinforce, but which casual ignorance can just as easily destroy. Some recent commercially produced versions of 'Tam o' Shanter' cannot even pronounce the most basic sounds of Scots, much less catch the subtleties of the what is now the oldest spoken form of its first cousin, English. Most schoolchildren appear to leave school ignorant of Scottish literature and history. There is an intellectual vogue for denigrating *Burns nichts*, although these are occasions where at best people with no specialist knowledge of the poet can find out more and thoroughly enjoy themselves at the same time. Indifference and ignorance is also the penalty we pay if we turn Burns into a mysterious and half-understood deity. The tradition to which Robert Burns gave glorious voice is a sturdy plant that will thrive on rough handling, but will wither in either a drought or an overheated temple. What is it worth? Anyone who has heard Jean Redpath or Rod Patterson sing the songs of Robert Burns will understand Fletcher of Saltoun's conclusion:

If a man were permitted to make all the ballads, he need not care who should make the laws of a nation.

Reading the inscription beneath D.W. Stevenson's relief of 'The Cotter's Saturday Night':

From scenes like these, old Scotia's grandeur springs.

At the heart of the poem is a vision of the human dignity that is in all people.

PHOTO: GAVIN SPROTT

INDEX

'A Man's a Man for a' that' 107, 162, 164
'A Poet's Welcome to his Love-Begotten Daughter' 62
Act of Assembly 1649 82
'Address of Beelzebub' 98, 114, 127
'Ae Fond Kiss' 8, 10, 127
Agricultural Revolution 17, 26–27, 29, 34, 40, 111, 150
agriculture see Agricultural Revolution, cotters, estates, farming, farming community, tenant farmers
Ainslie, Bob 63
ale 30, 40–41, 82
Alexander, William 76
Allan, David 18, 79, 81
Alloway: Burns Cottage 27–29; Burns Monument 74
Alloway kirkyard 12
American colonies 96, 97–99
American Revolution 97–99
Anderson, Robert 19
Angellier, Auguste 178–179
armorial bearings 15–16
Armour, James 133
Armour, Jean: 8, 17, 23, 59, 61, 63, 64, 65, 66, 67–69, 131, 134, 135, 142, 143, 154, 175; portraits 65
'Auld Lang Syne' 79, 89, 178
Ayton, Colonel 17

'Ballad on the American War' 97
Barke, James 174–175
Baron Court 38
Begg, Isabella Burns 143
beggars 38–40
Bervie kirkyard 12
'Birthday Ode' 115
Black Stool ('creepy chair') 63
Blacklock, Dr 137
Blair, Dr Hugh 137
Blair, Helen 59
Blake, William 139
Borthwick Johnstone, William 13, 15
Boston, Thomas 74
Boswell, Alexander 73–74, 143
Boswell, James 73, 95
Bough, Sam 159
Braxfield, Robert Macqueen, Lord 99, 100, 101
Brow Well 134–135, 144–145
Brunswick, Duke of 102
Buchanan, George 96–97
Buego, John 17
Burghs 40–41

Burke, Edmund 100
Burnes, Agnes, née Brown 12, 27, 56, 59
Burnes, James (great-grandfather) 12, 130
Burnes, James (uncle) 26
Burnes, or Burness family 12, 26, 60, 130
Burnes, Robert 12, 26
Burnes, William 12, 15, 26–27, 29, 42, 43, 45, 46, 80, 81, 92, 100, 108
Burns bicentenary postage stamps 187
Burns Clubs 146, 162,163 see also Burns Federation
Burns Federation 146, 162
Burns, Gilbert 12, 21, 23, 24, 41, 42, 43, 45, 75, 140, 142, 146
Burns industry 169–170
Burns, Isabel 27
Burns, James (son) 143
Burns, Jean see Jean Armour
Burns Mausoleum 16, 143
Burns nichts 146, 187
Burns, Robert: and animals 25, 35; appearance, dress and manner 14–15, 17–21, 94, 125–126; armorial bearings 15–16; biographies 135–143, 145–146, 151–152, 170–175; birth and birthplace 27–29; centenary celebrations 163, 170; and dancing 81; death and funeral 135, 136; depression 174; and drink 23–24, 82–83, 132, 133, 152, 182, 183; epitaphs 132; Exciseman 119–126; farmer 21, 23, 44, 45; Freemason 41, 94–95, 96, 97, 100; and friendship 128–131; and Gaelic culture 127; graffitist 123–125; health 43–44, 125, 132, 134–135, 182; Jacobitism 115–117, 123–124; and language 73, 74–75; letters quoted 9,10–11, 16, 44, 46, 53, 56, 63, 65, 66, 67, 72, 77, 79, 81, 84, 85, 86, 87, 100–101, 104, 115, 116, 119, 125, 126, 131, 134; literary admirers 159–161; literary influences 46, 53, 72, 73, 74, 75, 76, 77; on marriage 65–66, 67, 69; 19th century view 148–149, 150, 151–152; patriotism 113–114, 115–117; political philosophy 52; politics 100–107; popularity 73, 75–76, 109–110, 143; portraits 13,

17–18, 19, 20, 161; posthumous reputation 134, 137–143, 144–149, 151–152, 159; proposed emigration 154; and poverty 14, 39–40, 166–168; quoted on his deathbed 17; recent studies 186–187 see also Dr James Mackay; religion and moral philosophy 46, 52, 53; reputation abroad and translations 176–183; and Scots military tradition 117–119; 'sensibility' 53–54; songs, ballads and music 59, 69, 76–80, 81, 83–89; statues 160, 161–162; and superstition and the supernatural 56–59; temperament 21–23; travels 109, 112, 126–128; and women 24, 59, 60, 62–69
Burns, Robert (son) 143–144
Burns, Sarah 65
Burns, William (son) 143

'Ca' the Yowes' 78–79, 89
Cairney, John 175–176
Calvinism 17, 50, 51–52, 96
Cameron, May 66
Cameronians 47
Campbell, Margaret see 'Highland Mary'
'Can ye Labour Lea' 59
Carlyle, Thomas 16, 74, 77, 94, 111, 137, 139, 142
Carnegie, Andrew 161
Carron Ironworks 120
Carse, Alexander 29, 30
Carswell, Catherine 153, 170–174, 179
Chalmers, Peggy, or Margaret (Mrs Lewis Hay) 65, 67
Chambers, Robert 142–143, 145, 150, 151
Chartism 168
cheese-making 67, 69
Claim of Right 1690 91
Clarinda see Agnes McLehose
Clark, William 21, 23
Clarke, Stephen 85
Clow, Jenny 8, 66
Cockburn, Lord 73
'Come Rede Me, Dame' 64
Constable, Lady Winifred Maxwell 115
cottages: Burns Memorial Cottages 165; Burns's views 163; construction and interior 27–31; Rosebery's improvements 163–164

189

HMSO

HMSO Bookshops
71 Lothian Road, Edinburgh EH3 9AZ
0131-228 4181 Fax 0131-229 2734
49 High Holborn, London WC1V 6HB
(counter service only)
0171-873 0011 Fax 0171-831 1326
68-69 Bull Street, Birmingham B4 6AD
0121-236 9696 Fax 0121-236 9699
33 Wine Street, Bristol BS1 2BQ
0117 9264306 Fax 0117 9294515
9-21 Princess Street, Manchester M60 8AS
0161-834 7201 Fax 0161-833 0634
16 Arthur Street, Belfast BT1 4GD
01232 238451 Fax 01232 235401
The HMSO Oriel Bookshop
The Friary, Cardiff CF1 4AA
01222 395548 Fax 01222 384347

Published by HMSO and available from:

HMSO Publications Centre
(Mail, fax and telephone orders only)
PO Box 276, London SW8 5DT
Telephone orders 0171-873 9090
General enquiries 0171-873 0011
(queuing system in operation for both numbers)
Fax orders 0171-873 8200

HMSO's Accredited Agents
(see Yellow Pages)

and through good booksellers

Printed in Great Britain for HMSO Scotland by CC No. 70343, 35c, 05/96